UPDATED EDITION

Guess What!

Activity Book 1

with Digital Pack

British English

Susan Rivers

Series Editor: Lesley Koustaff

Shaftesbury Road, Cambridge CB2 8EA, United Kingdom

One Liberty Plaza, 20th Floor, New York, NY 10006, USA

477 Williamstown Road, Port Melbourne, VIC 3207, Australia

314–321, 3rd Floor, Plot 3, Splendor Forum, Jasola District Centre, New Delhi – 110025, India

103 Penang Road, #05–06/07, Visioncrest Commercial, Singapore 238467

Cambridge University Press & Assessment is a department of the University of Cambridge.

We share the University's mission to contribute to society through the pursuit of education, learning and research at the highest international levels of excellence.

www.cambridge.org
Information on this title: www.cambridge.org/9781009798327

First published 2014
Updated edition 2024

20 19 18 17 16 15 14 13 12 11 10 9 8 7 6 5 4 3

Printed in the Netherlands by Wilco BV

A catalogue record for this publication is available from the British Library

ISBN 978-1-009-79832-7 Activity Book with Digital Pack Level 1
ISBN 978-1-009-79829-7 Pupil's Book with eBook Level 1
ISBN 978-1-009-79838-9 Teacher's Book with Digital Pack Level 1
ISBN 978-1-107-52697-6 Flashcards Level 1

Additional resources for this publication at www.cambridge.org/guesswhatue

Contents

Hello!

1 Look and match.

1

a

b

2

c

3

d

4

2 Ask and answer with a friend.

1 Hello, I'm Mandy. What's your name?

2 Hello, I'm Jack.

3 This is Penny.

4 Hello, Penny.

Listen and stick.

Listen and number.

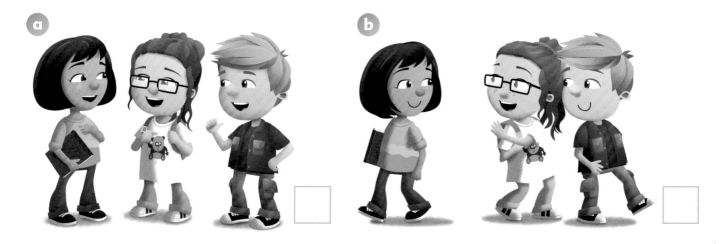

5 Think **What's next? Draw a line.**

1 2 4 6 2 4 6 2 4 ← | 10

2 8 9 10 8 9 10 8 9 → | 6

3 3 5 7 3 5 7 3 5 | 4

4 6 5 4 6 5 4 6 5 | 3

5 1 8 3 1 8 3 1 8 | 7

6 0.09 **Listen and write the numbers in the pictures.**

1

2

3

4

7 🎧 0.12 **Listen and colour.**

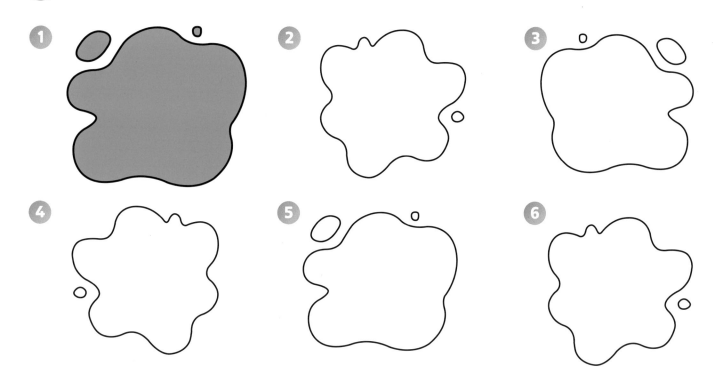

8 (About Me) **Look. Then draw and say.**

How old are you?

I'm …

What's your favourite colour?

My favourite colour's …

My picture dictionary → Go to page 84: Tick the words you know and trace.

9 🎧 0.14 Listen and tick ✓.

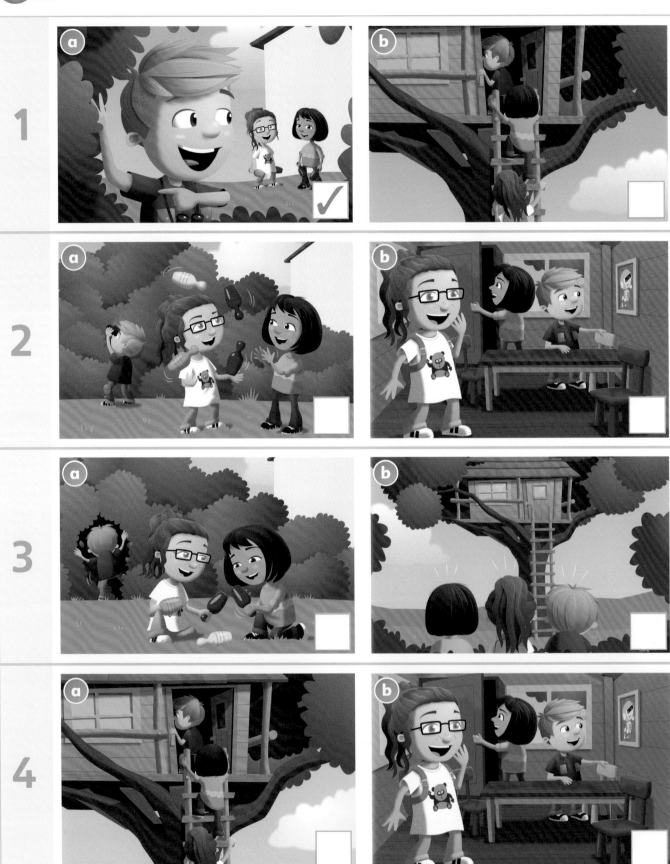

10 **What's missing? Look and draw. Then stick.**

I'm curious.

11 **Trace the letters.**

A pink and purple panda.

12 🎧 0.17 **Listen and circle the *p* words.**

①    ②    ③ 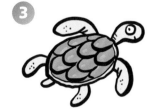   ④

What **colour** is it?

1 🎧 0.19 **Listen and colour.**

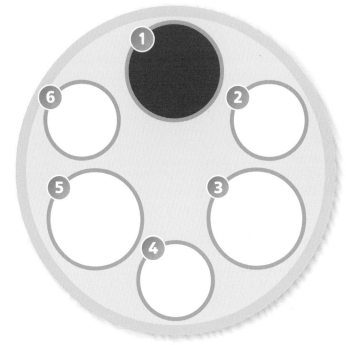

2 **Look and colour.**

1 +  =

2 + =

3  +  =

Evaluation

1 Follow the lines. Then trace and say.

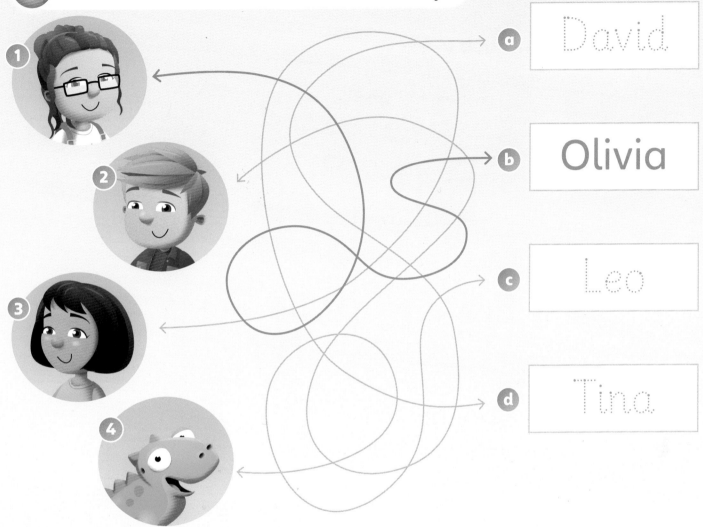

a David

b Olivia

c Leo

d Tina

2 What's your favourite part? Use your stickers.

story   song   video

3 Puzzle Trace the colour.

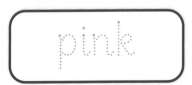

pink

Then go to page 93 and colour the Hello! unit pieces.

1 🎧 1.04 **Listen and tick ✓.**

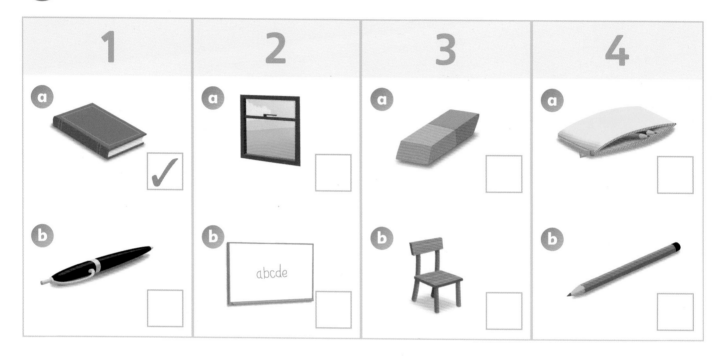

1	2	3	4
a ✓	**a** ☐	**a** ☐	**a** ☐
b ☐	**b** abcde ☐	**b** ☐	**b** ☐

2 **Look and match.**

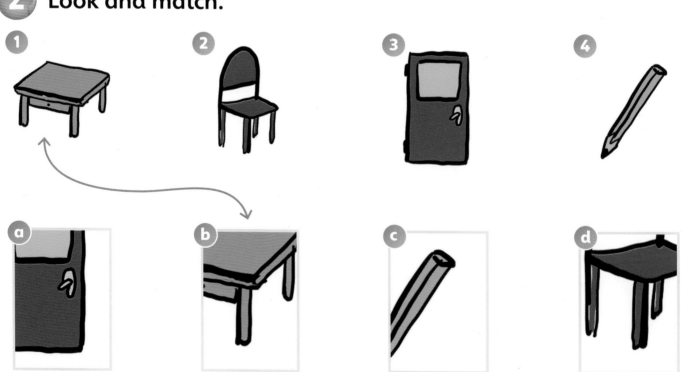

3 🎧1.06 Listen and stick.

1
2
3

4
5

4 Think What's next? Draw a line.

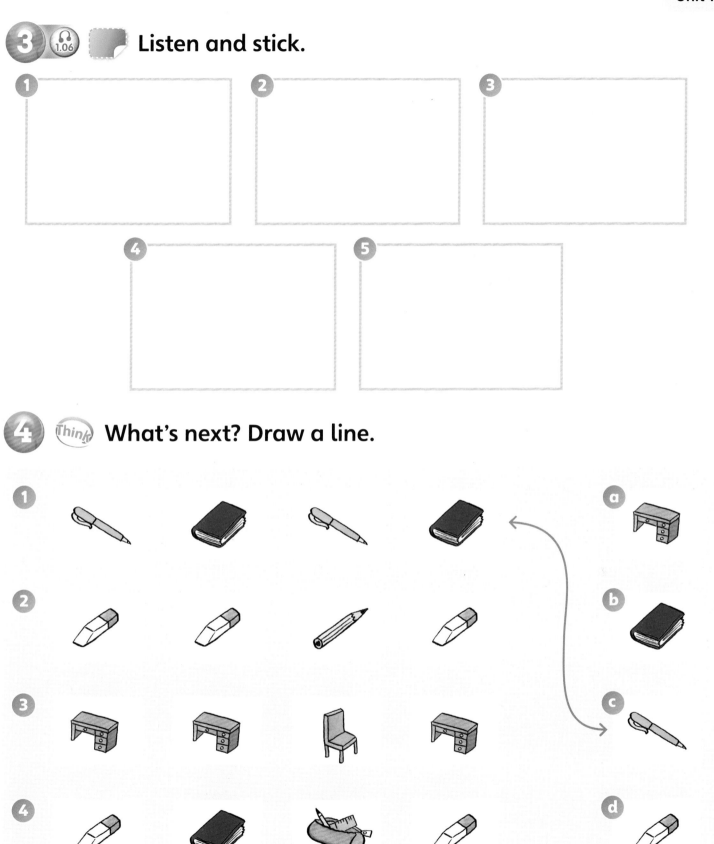

My picture dictionary ➔ Go to page 85: Tick the words you know and trace.

Vocabulary **13**

5 Look and count. Write the number.

2

6 Ask and answer about your classroom.

How many rubbers can you see?   Three.

7 🎧 1.11 Listen and tick ✓ or cross ✗.

1

✗

2

3

4

8 Think Circle the different one.

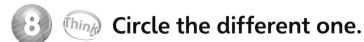

1 a  b

2 a  b  c  d

10 **What's missing? Look and draw. Then stick.**

I'm friendly.

11 **Trace the letters.**

A bear with
a blue book.

12 (1.16) **Listen and circle the *b* words.**

1

2

abcde

3

4

Value   Pronunciation: *b*   **17**

What **material** is it?

1 Look and match.

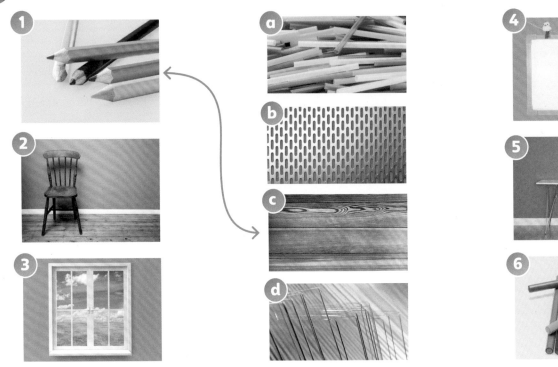

2 🎧 1.18 Listen and tick ✓.

Evaluation

1 **Look and trace. Then say.**

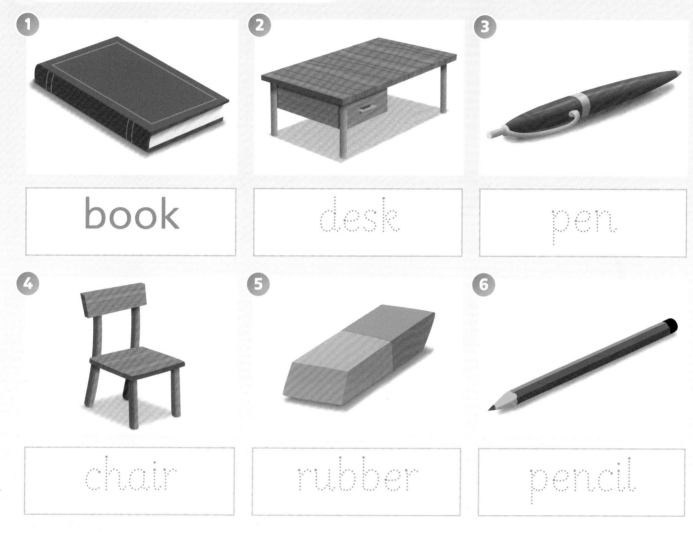

1 book

2 desk

3 pen

4 chair

5 rubber

6 pencil

2 What's your favourite part? Use your stickers.

story song video

3 Puzzle **Trace the colour.**

red

Then go to page 93 and colour the Unit 1 pieces.

2 Toys

1 🎧 2.04 **Listen and tick ✓ .**

	1	2	3	4
a	✓			
b				

2 **Look, match and say.** 1 kite

3 **Listen and stick.**

1
2
3
4
5

4 **Think** **Look and circle the toys.**

My picture dictionary → Go to page 86: Tick the words you know and trace.

5 🎧 2.09 **Listen and tick ✓ or cross ✗.**

1 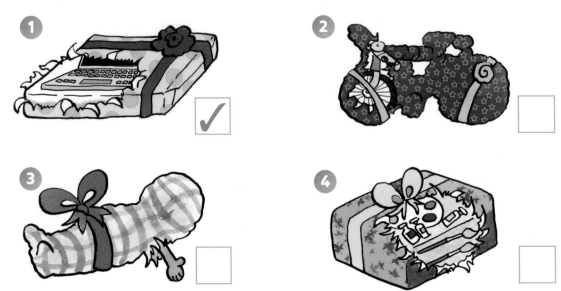 ✓

2 ☐

3 ☐

4 ☐

6 (About Me) **Draw your favourite toy and say.**

What's this?

It's a …

Listen and number the pictures.

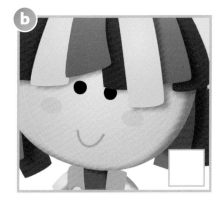

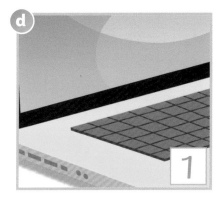

1

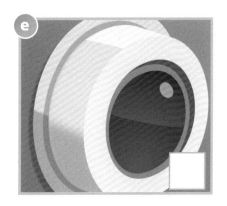

 Listen and draw the pictures.

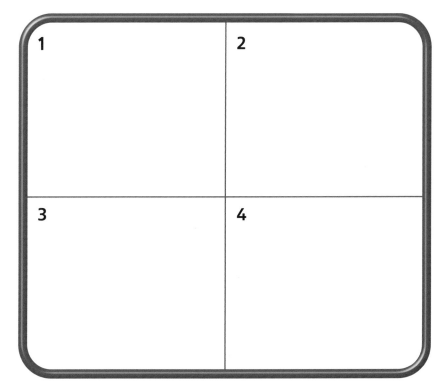

1	2
3	4

10 **What's missing? Look and draw. Then stick.**

I'm polite.

a

b

c

11 **Trace the letters.**

A turtle with two teddy bears.

12 **Listen and circle the _t_ words.**

 1

 2

 3

 4

Is it electric?

1 🎧 2.19 **Listen and tick ✓ (electric) or cross ✗ (not electric).**

1 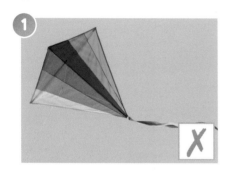 ✗

2

3

4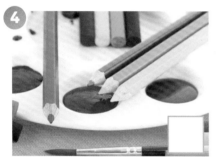

5

6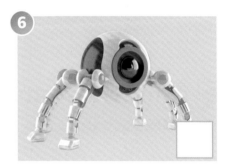

2 **Look at Activity 1 and draw.**

Electric	Not electric

Evaluation

1 Look and trace. Then say.

1

kite

2

robot

3

ball

4

bike

5

doll

6

camera

2  What's your favourite part? Use your stickers.

story   song   video

3 Puzzle Trace the colour.

green

Then go to page 93 and colour the Unit 2 pieces.

Review **Units 1 and 2**

1 Look and say. Find and circle.

2 🎧 2.21 **Listen and number the pictures.**

a

b

c

d

1

e

f

7

3 Family

1 Trace the words and match.

1. mum
2. dad
3. sister
4. brother
5. grandma

2 Look and write the number.

1 cousin   **2** uncle   **3** grandpa   **4** aunt

Listen and stick.

1. 2. 3. 4. 5.

  Read, look and tick ✓.

1. **dad**

☐ ☐ ✓

2. **aunt**

☐ ☐ ☐

3. **grandma**

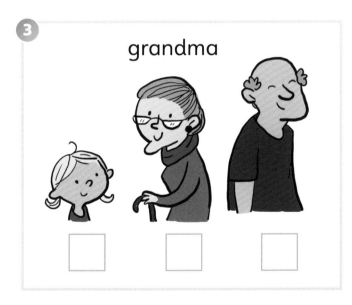

☐ ☐ ☐

4. **brother**

☐ ☐ ☐

My picture dictionary → Go to page 87: Tick the words you know and trace.

Vocabulary **31**

5 Look, read and match.

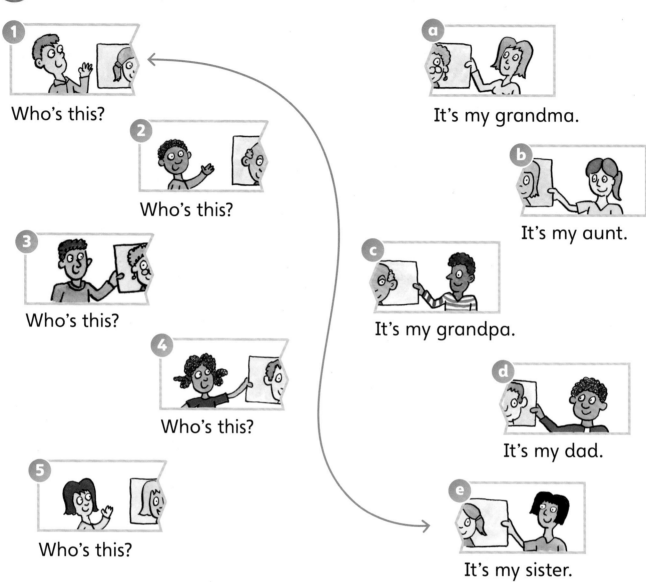

1 Who's this?

2 Who's this?

3 Who's this?

4 Who's this?

5 Who's this?

a It's my grandma.

b It's my aunt.

c It's my grandpa.

d It's my dad.

e It's my sister.

6 (About Me) Draw a member of your family. Then ask and answer with a friend.

Who's this?

It's my ...

7 **3.11 Listen, read and tick ✓.**

1

my brother ☐

my cousin ✓

2

my mum ☐

my aunt ☐

3

my mum ☐

my grandma ☐

4

my sister ☐

my cousin ☐

5

my cousin ☐

my aunt ☐

6

my dad ☐

my uncle ☐

8 **Look, read and circle the correct word.**

1 Who's **this / that**?
It's my uncle.

2 Who's **this / that**?
It's my cousin.

3 Who's **this / that**?
It's my grandpa.

4 Who's **this / that**?
It's my sister.

10 **What's missing? Look and draw. Then stick.**

I love my family.

11 **Trace the letters.**

A dolphin in a red desk.

12 **Listen and circle the *d* words.**

1

2

3

4

1 (3.18) **Listen and write the number.**

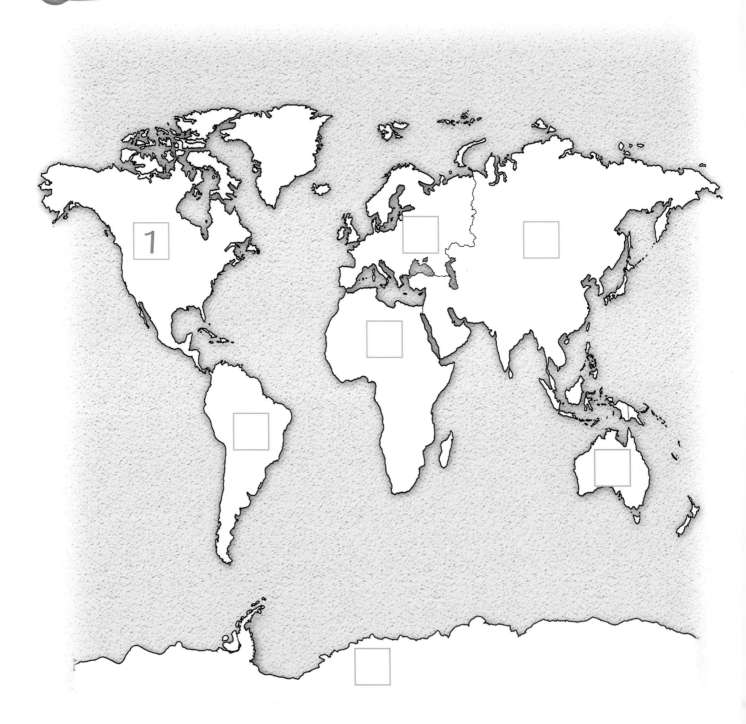

2 (3.19) **Look at the map again. Listen and colour.**

Evaluation

1 **Read and trace. Then circle and say.**

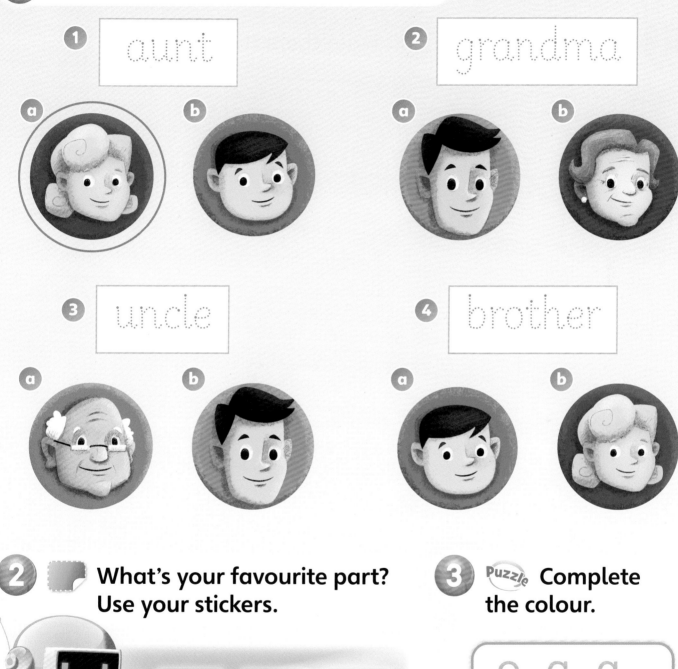

1 aunt
a b

2 grandma
a b

3 uncle
a b

4 brother
a b

2 **What's your favourite part? Use your stickers.**

story song video

3 Puzzle **Complete the colour.**

o_a_g_

Then go to page 93 and colour the Unit 3 pieces.

1 Look at the picture and write the letter.

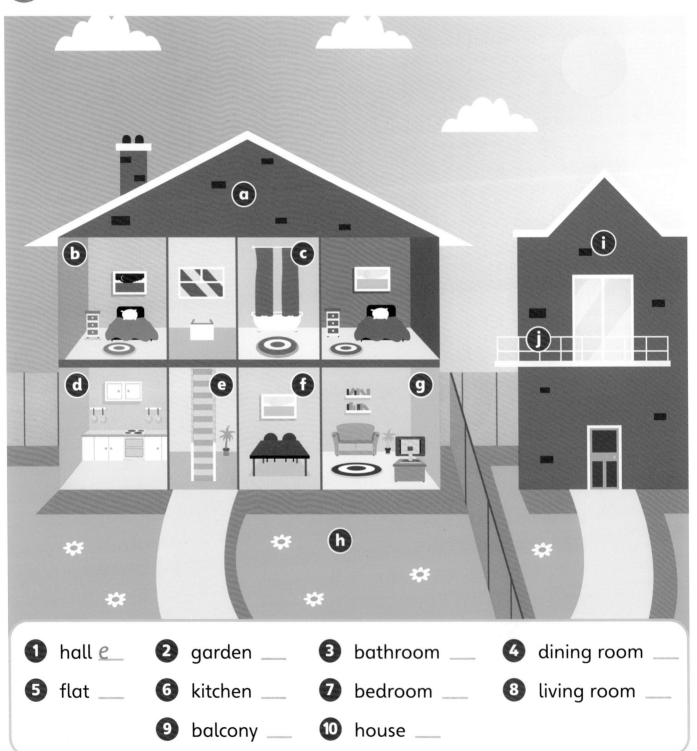

1 hall _e_	**2** garden __	**3** bathroom __	**4** dining room __
5 flat __	**6** kitchen __	**7** bedroom __	**8** living room __
	9 balcony __	**10** house __	

2 **Listen and stick.**

1	2	3

4	5	6

3 **Look, read and circle the correct word.**

1 (kitchen) / dining room

2 hall / living room

3 bedroom / balcony

4 kitchen / bathroom

5 hall / garden

6 balcony / dining room

My picture dictionary Go to page 88: Tick the words you know and trace.

Look, read and match.

Where's your aunt?

I'm in the garden.

Where's your cousin?

She's in the hall.

Where's your mum?

She's in the bathroom.

Where are you?

He's in the bedroom.

  Draw yourself. Ask and answer with a friend.

Where are you?

I'm in …

6 Listen and write the number.

1   2  3  4  5

7 Draw the objects in the picture. Ask and answer.

Where's the _____ ?   It's _____ ?

8 🎧 4.12 Listen and number.

9 **What's missing? Look and draw. Then stick.**

I look after things.

10 **Trace the letters.**

An ant with an apple.

11 **Listen and circle the *a* words.**

 **1**

 **2**

 3

 **4**

What shape is it?

1 Look and colour the shapes.

2 What's next? Match, then draw and colour the shapes.

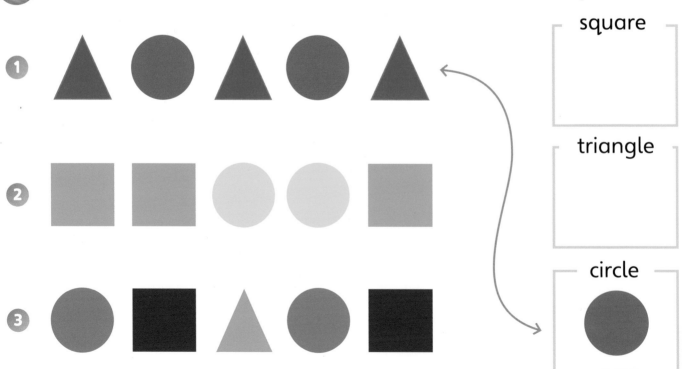

square

triangle

circle

Evaluation

1 Read and trace. Then circle and say.

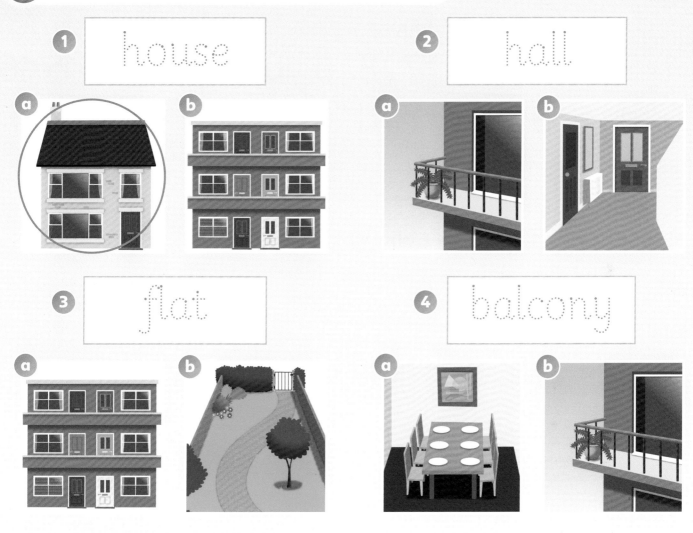

1 house

2 hall

3 flat

4 balcony

2 What's your favourite part? Use your stickers.

3 Puzzle Complete the colour.

y _ l _ o _

Then go to page 93 and colour the Unit 4 pieces.

Review Units 3 and 4

1 Write the words and match.

1	2	3	4	5	6	7	8	9	10	11	12	13	14	15	16
u	a	t	b	s	c	r	d	o	e	n	g	m	h	k	i

1 b r o t h e r
   4 7 9 3 14 10 7

2 _ _ _ _ _ _ _
   15 16 3 6 14 10 11

3 _ _ _ _ _ _ _
   12 7 2 11 8 13 2

4 _ _ _ _ _ _
   12 2 7 8 10 11

5 _ _ _
   8 2 8

6 _ _ _ _ _
   14 9 1 5 10

a
b
c
d
e
f

46

2 Read and match the questions with the answers.

1 Where's the computer? _c_
2 Is that your cousin? ___
3 Who's that? ___
4 Where's your mum? ___

a She's in the living room.
b No, it isn't. It's my sister.
c It's on the desk.
d It's my sister.

3 Circle the correct words and write.

mum   bedroom   grandma   ~~under~~

1

What's / (Where's) the doll?
It's ___under___ the bed.

2

Who's / Where's this?
It's my _____.

3

Who / Where are you?
I'm in my _____.

4

Is that / Who's your aunt?
No, it isn't. It's my
_____.

47

5 My body

1 **Read and circle the correct word.**

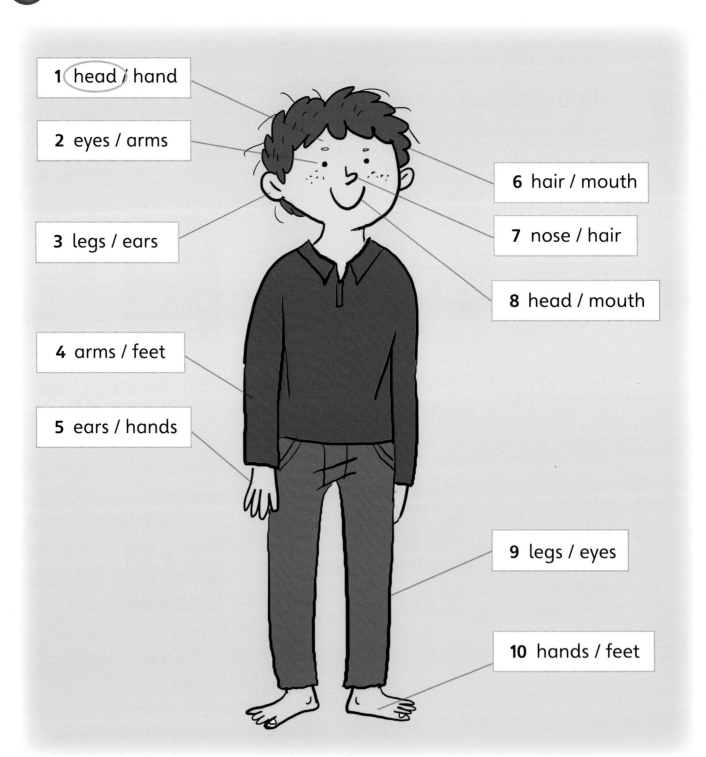

1 (head) / hand

2 eyes / arms

3 legs / ears

4 arms / feet

5 ears / hands

6 hair / mouth

7 nose / hair

8 head / mouth

9 legs / eyes

10 hands / feet

2   **Listen and stick.**

1	2	3
4	5	6

3 **Look at the picture. Find and circle the words.**

h	e	a	d	e	p	n
l	e	g	l	a	l	o
h	h	k	o	r	j	s
a	a	e	r	t	y	e
i	r	w	h	a	n	d
r	m	o	u	t	h	n
q	n	v	f	e	e	t

My picture dictionary ➡ Go to page 89: Tick the words you know and trace.

 **4** **5.08** Listen and tick ✓.

1	2	3
a	a	a
b ✓	b	b
c	c	c

5 (Think) **What's different? Circle the word.**

(eyes) / ears

feet / hands

legs / arms

mouth / nose

6 Look, read and tick ✓.

1

Have you got hair?

☐ Yes, I have. ✓ No, I haven't.

2

Have you got two arms?

☐ Yes, I have. ☐ No, I haven't.

3

Have you got four legs?

☐ Yes, I have. ☐ No, I haven't.

4

Have you got one nose?

☐ Yes, I have. ☐ No, I haven't.

7 (About Me) Draw a robot. Then complete the sentences.

I've got _____

_____ .

I haven't got _____

_____ .

9 What's missing? Look and draw. Then stick.

a

b

c

I'm clean.

10 Trace the letters.

An iguana
with pink ink.

11 5.14 Listen and circle the *i* words.

1

2

3

4

What sense is it?

1 **Look, read and match.**

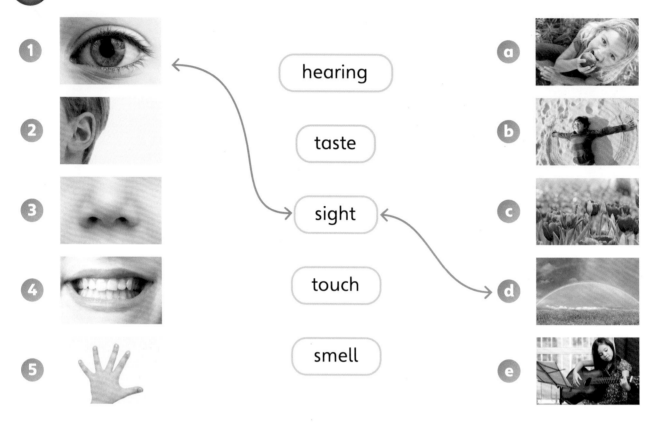

2 **Look and tick ✓.**

	👁	👂	👃	😁	✋
🌻	✓				
🥁					
🧸					
🍦					
🌊					

Evaluation

1 Look, match and trace. Then read and say.

head

feet

ears

nose

2 What's your favourite part?
Use your stickers.

story   song   video

3 Puzzle **Complete the colour.**

b _ u _

Then go to page
93 and colour
the Unit 5 pieces.

6 Food

1 Look and write the word.

1
k m l i

milk

2
p e a l p

_____

3
g e g

_____

4
c e h s e e

_____

5
a e w r t

_____

6
a a a n n b

_____

2 Complete the words and match.

1 jui_c_e   **2** o _ a n g e   **3** b _ e a d   **4** c _ i c k _ n

a    **b**    **c**    **d**

Listen and stick.

1

2

3

4

  Look and write the words.

cheese	an apple	juice	bread	water
a banana	an egg	an orange	chicken	milk

We eat ...

1 _cheese_

2 _____

3 _____

4 _____

5 _____

6 _____

7 _____

We drink ...

1 _____

2 _____

3 _____

 My picture dictionary ➔ Go to page 90: Tick the words you know and trace.

5 6.08 **Listen and tick ✓ or cross ✗.**

1			✓	✗
2				
3				
4				

6 **Look, read and circle.**

 **1** I like / (don't like) juice.

 **2** I like / **don't like** oranges.

 **3** I like / **don't like** bread.

 **4** I like / **don't like** water.

 **5** I like / **don't like** apples.

 **6** I like / **don't like** eggs.

7 Look, read and tick ✓.

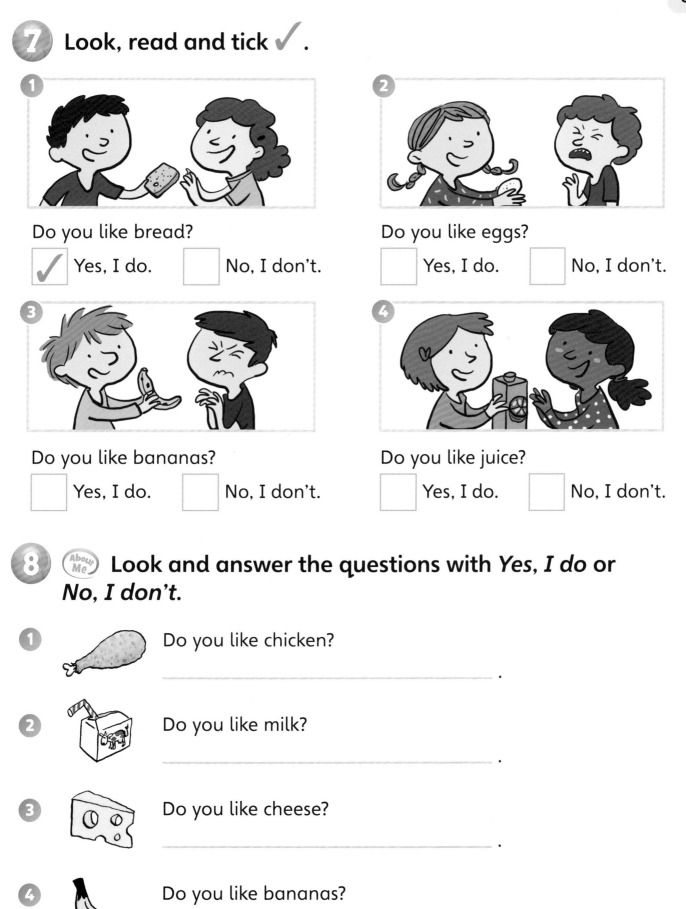

1

Do you like bread?

✓ Yes, I do. ☐ No, I don't.

2

Do you like eggs?

☐ Yes, I do. ☐ No, I don't.

3

Do you like bananas?

☐ Yes, I do. ☐ No, I don't.

4

Do you like juice?

☐ Yes, I do. ☐ No, I don't.

8 (About Me) Look and answer the questions with *Yes, I do* or *No, I don't.*

1 Do you like chicken?

_____ .

2 Do you like milk?

_____ .

3 Do you like cheese?

_____ .

4 Do you like bananas?

_____ .

9 🎧 6.11 Listen, look and match.

10 **What's missing? Look and draw. Then stick.**

I'm patient.

11 **Trace the letters.**

An elephant
with ten eggs.

12 6.14 **Listen and circle the e words.**

1

2

3

4

Where is **food** from?

1 **Look and tick ✓ or cross ✗.**

Plants

✓

Animals

2 **Look, read and circle.**

1

(plant) / animal

2

plant / animal

3

plant / animal

4

plant / animal

5

plant / animal

6

plant / animal

Evaluation

1 **Look, match and write. Then read and say.**

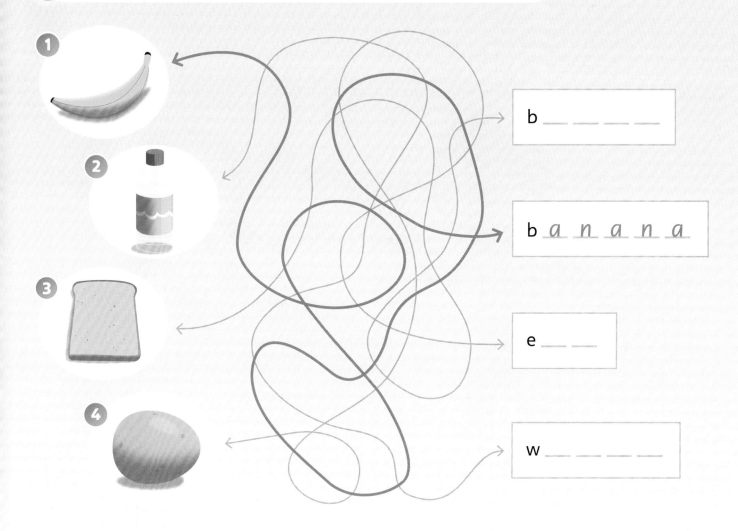

1 b _ _ _ _ _ _

b _a_ _n_ _a_ _n_ _a_

e _ _ _ _

w _ _ _ _ _ _

2 **What's your favourite part? Use your stickers.**

story   song   video

3 Puzzle **Write the colour.**

p e u l r p _ _ _ _ _ _

Then go to page 93 and colour the Unit 6 pieces.

Review Units 5 and 6

1 Look and write.

cheese	~~arms~~	water	mouth
bread	legs	orange	nose

1 *arms*

2 _____

3 _____

4 _____

5 _____

6 _____

7 _____

8 _____

2 Read and match.

1 I like   a like juice.
2 I've got   b two ears.
3 I don't   c chicken.
4 I haven't   d got two heads.

3 Write the question. Then tick ✓.

1

you / three / Have / got / hands?

Have you got three hands?

☐ Yes, I have.   ✓ No, I haven't.

2

like / eggs / you / Do?

_____

☐ Yes, I do.   ☐ No, I don't.

3

got / two / you / Have / ears?

_____

☐ Yes, I have.   ☐ No, I haven't.

4

you / Do / milk / like?

_____

☐ Yes, I do.   ☐ No, I don't.

1 Look, read and circle the word.

swim / (sing)

climb / paint

dance / draw

ride a bike / play football

2 Look at the pictures. Find and circle the words.

runswimjumppaintclimb(dance)

3 🎧 7.05 Listen and stick.

1	2	3
4	5	6

4 Think Read and circle the object.

1 dance

2 draw

3 sing

4 swim

My picture dictionary → Go to page 91: Tick the words you know and trace.

5 🎧 7.08 **Listen and circle the picture.**

1

2

3

4

6 **Look and write** *can* **or** *can't.*

1 I ___can___ run.

2 I _____ draw.

3 I _____ climb.

4 I _____ dance.

7 Look, read and tick ✓.

1

Can you swim?

☐ Yes, I can. ✓ No, I can't.

2

Can you jump?

☐ Yes, I can. ☐ No, I can't.

3

Can you ride a bike?

☐ Yes, I can. ☐ No, I can't.

4

Can you dance?

☐ Yes, I can. ☐ No, I can't.

8 (About Me) Complete the table. Ask three friends and tick ✓.

Name	🎤	🎨	🚲
1 _Me_			
2			
3			
4			

Can you sing?   Yes, I can. / No, I can't.

9 **7.11** Listen and number.

10 **What's missing? Look and draw. Then stick.**

I help my friends.

11 **Trace the letters.**

An umbrella
bird can jump.

12 7.14 **Listen and circle the *u* words.**

1  2   3  4

What's the number?

1 **Think and write the answer. Then colour.**

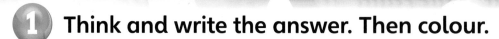

1 1 + 1 = [2] red   **2** 2 + 4 = [ ] blue

3 3 + 6 = [ ] orange   **4** 10 – 2 = [ ] purple

5 5 – 2 = [ ] green   **6** 8 – 4 = [ ] yellow

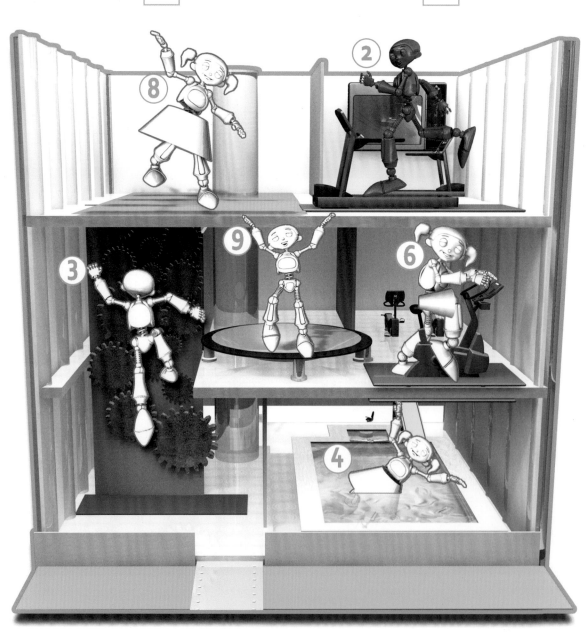

Evaluation

1 **Look and write the word. Then read and say.**

1. r u n

2. _ _ _ _ _ _

3. _ _ _ _ _

4. _ _ _ _

5. _ _ _ _

6. _ _ _

2 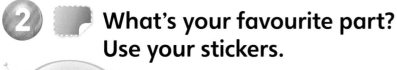 **What's your favourite part? Use your stickers.**

story   song   video

3 **Puzzle** **Write the colour.**

e y r g _____

Then go to page 93 and colour the Unit 7 pieces.

Animals

1 Look and match.

 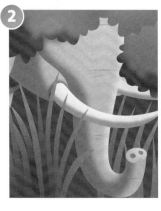  

a crocodile **b** giraffe **c** spider **d** elephant

2 Look and write the word.

1

n l o i

lion

2

b e r z a

_____

3

i d b r

_____

4

o i p h p

_____

5

m y o e k n

_____

6

e a k n s

_____

3 🎧 8.05 📑 **Listen and stick.**

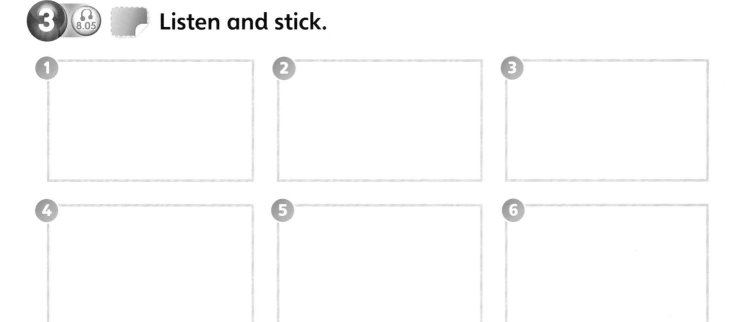

4 Think **Write the words. Circle the animals with four legs.**

snake   spider   bird   ~~zebra~~   elephant   giraffe   hippo   lion

1. zebra
2. _____
3. _____
4. _____
5. _____
6. _____
7. _____
8. _____

My picture dictionary → Go to page 92: Tick the words you know and trace.

5 **Look and match the opposites.**

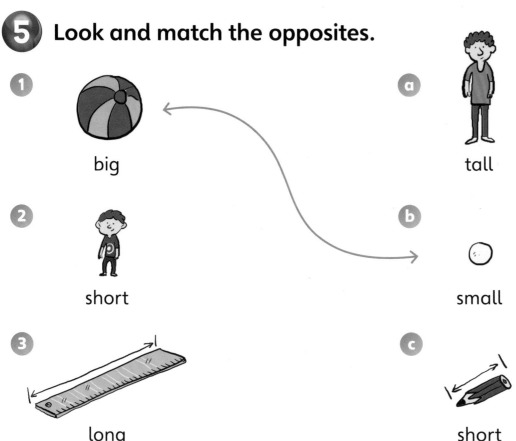

1 big

2 short

3 long

a tall

b small

c short

6 **Look, read and complete the sentences.**

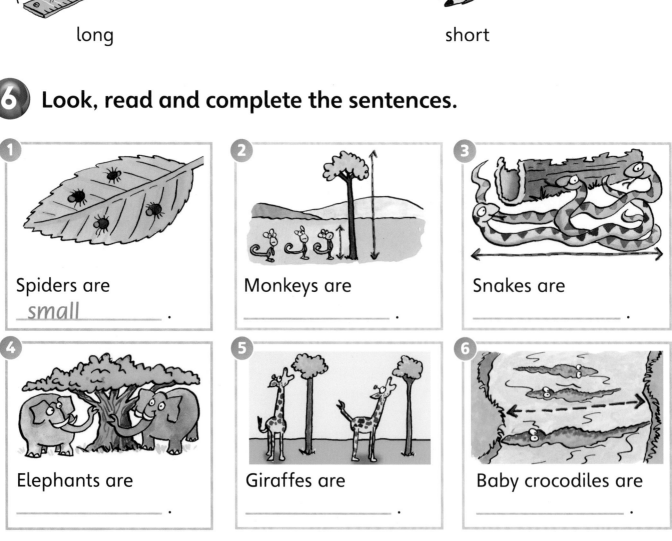

1 Spiders are _small_ .

2 Monkeys are _____ .

3 Snakes are _____ .

4 Elephants are _____ .

5 Giraffes are _____ .

6 Baby crocodiles are _____ .

7 **Look and read. Circle the correct sentences.**

Spiders have got wings.

Elephants have got long trunks.

Hippos have got long necks.

Monkeys have got long tails.

8 **Look and write.**

| big teeth | long tails | ~~small wings~~ | long necks | short legs |

1 Birds have got _small_ _wings_ .

2 Zebras have got _____ _____ .

3 Hippos have got _____ _____ .

4 Giraffes have got _____ _____ .

5 Birds have got _____ _____ .

9 **Ask and answer with a friend.**

What are your favourite animals?   Elephants.

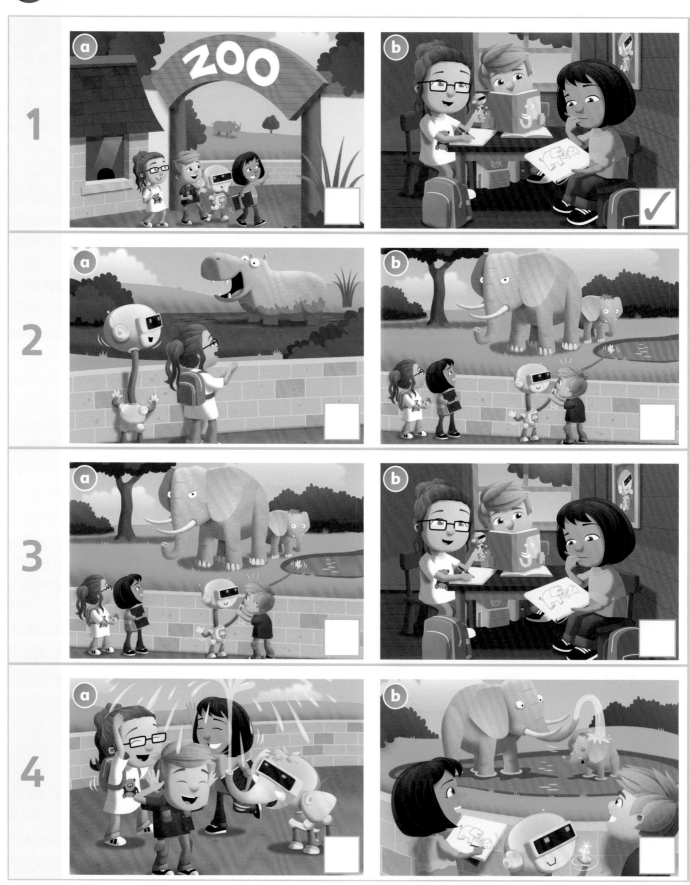

11 **What's missing? Look and draw. Then stick.**

I respect animals.

12 **Trace the letters.**

An octopus in
an orange box.

13 (8.14) **Listen and circle the o words.**

1

2

3

4

How do **animals** move?

1 **Read and complete. Then number the pictures.**

| slither | ~~walk~~ | fly | walk |

1 An elephant can ___walk___ .   **2** A snake can _____ .
3 A bird can _____ .   **4** A giraffe can _____ .

2 **Look at Activity 1 and circle the answers.**

1 Can a snake fly?   Yes, it can. / No, it can't.
2 Can an elephant walk?   Yes, it can. / No, it can't.
3 Can a bird fly?   Yes, it can. / No, it can't.
4 Can a giraffe slither?   Yes, it can. / No, it can't.

Evaluation

1 **Look and write the word. Then read and say.**

1

z e b r a

2

_ _ _ _ _

3

_ _ _ _ _

4

_ _ _ _ _ _ _ _

5

_ _ _ _ _ _ _

6

_ _ _ _ _

2 **What's your favourite part? Use your stickers.**

story   song   video

3 Puzzle **Write the colour.**

l c k a b _____

Then go to page 93 and colour the Unit 8 pieces.

Review Units 7 and 8

1 Look and write. Then draw number 9.

1 z e b r a
2 _ a _ o t a l
3 s _ a
4 j
5 _ i _ p
6 _ n _ e
7 _ o _ e
8 _ a _ n

2 **Look and write.**

> football   small   long necks   a bike   ~~swim~~

1 Can you _swim_ ?
2 Birds are _____ .
3 I can play _____ .
4 Giraffes have got _____ .
5 I can't ride _____ .

3 **Look, read and circle the words.**

1  (Snakes) / **spiders** are long.

2  I **can** / **can't** sing.

3  Hippos **have got** / **haven't got** short tails.

4  I can **draw** / **dance**.

Hello!

blue ✓

green ☐

orange ☐

pink ☐

purple ☐

red ☐

yellow ☐

1 School

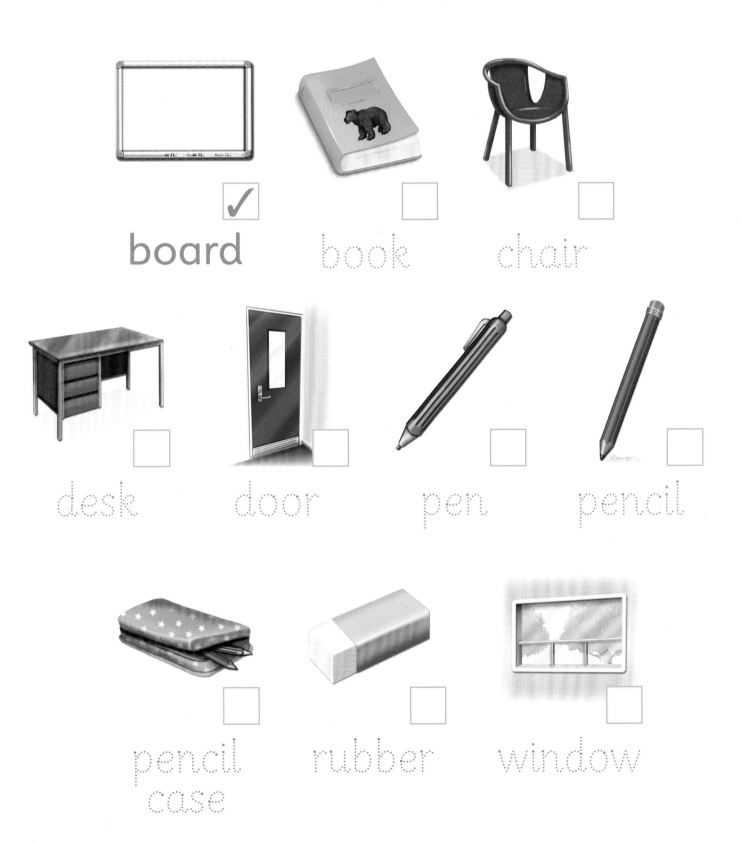

board ✓

book ☐

chair ☐

desk ☐

door ☐

pen ☐

pencil ☐

pencil case ☐

rubber ☐

window ☐

✓

art set

ball

bike

camera

computer

computer game

doll

kite

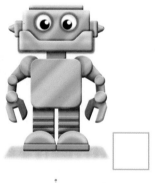

robot

teddy bear

aunt ✓

brother

cousin

dad

grandma

grandpa

mum

sister

uncle

balcony ✓

bathroom

bedroom

dining room

flat

garden

hall

house

kitchen

living room

arms ✓

ears

eyes

feet

head

hair

hands

legs

mouth

nose

6 Food

apple ✓

banana ☐

bread ☐

cheese ☐

chicken ☐

egg ☐

juice ☐

milk ☐

orange ☐

water ☐

7 My actions

climb ✓

dance

draw

jump

paint

play
football

ride a
bike

run

sing

swim

 ✓

bird

 ☐

crocodile

 ☐

elephant

 ☐

giraffe

 ☐

hippo

 ☐

lion

 ☐

monkey

 ☐

snake

 ☐

spider

 ☐

zebra

My puzzle

Guess What!

CAMBRIDGE
UNIVERSITY PRESS

University Printing House, Cambridge CB2 8BS, United Kingdom

One Liberty Plaza, 20th Floor, New York, NY 10006, USA

477 Williamstown Road, Port Melbourne, VIC 3207, Australia

314–321, 3rd Floor, Plot 3, Splendor Forum, Jasola District Centre, New Delhi – 110025, India

103 Penang Road, #05-06/07, Visioncrest Commercial, Singapore 238467

Cambridge University Press is part of the University of Cambridge.

It furthers the University's mission by disseminating knowledge in the pursuit of education, learning, and research at the highest international levels of excellence.

www.cambridge.org
Information on this title: www.cambridge.org/9781107557086

© Cambridge University Press 2016

First published 2016

24

Printed in Dubai by Oriental Press

A catalog record for this publication is available from the British Library

ISBN 978-1-107-55708-6 Workbook with Online Resources Level 5
ISBN 978-1-107-55703-1 Student's Book Level 5
ISBN 978-1-107-55714-7 Teacher's Book with DVD Level 5
ISBN 978-1-107-55720-8 Class Audio CDs Level 5
ISBN 978-1-107-55723-9 Presentation Plus DVD-ROM Level 5
ISBN 978-1-107-55726-0 Teacher's Resource and Tests CD-ROM Levels 5–6

Additional resources for this publication at www.cambridge.org/guesswhatamericanenglish

Guess What!

Workbook 5

with Online Resources

American English

Lynne Marie Robertson

Series Editor: Lesley Koustaff

Contents

Around the world

1 Look and write the words on the map.

> hinaC   lriBaz   het detiUn asettS   sisuaR   boloCaim
> xcMeoi   latIy   eraFnc   ~~hte Unedit modginK~~   naSip

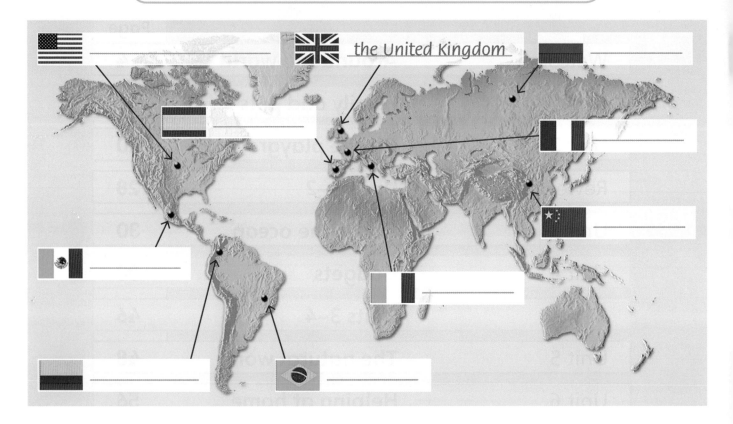

the United Kingdom

2 (Think) Look at activity 1. Answer the questions.

1 Which country doesn't have red in its flag?

    _____Brazil_____

2 Which two countries have red, white, and green flags?

    _____   _____

3 Which two countries have red and yellow flags?

    _____   _____

4 Which four countries have red, white, and blue flags?

    _____   _____   _____   _____

My picture dictionary → Go to page 84: Write the new words.

3 Complete the questions and answers. Use the words in parentheses.

Juan (Mexico)

Maria (Italy)

1 _Where_ are you _from_ ?
I'm _____from Mexico_____ .

2 _____'s she _____ ?
She's _____ .

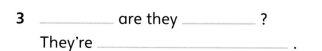
Bo and Hai (China)

Oliver (the United Kingdom)
and his father (Colombia)

3 _____ are they _____ ?
They're _____ .

4 _____'s Oliver's _____ ?
He's _____ .

4 Look at activity 3. Write the questions and answers.

1 _Is_ Oliver _from_ Mexico?   _No, he isn't._

2 _____ Bo and Hai _____ China?   _____

3 _____ Juan _____ Mexico?   _____

4 _____ Maria _____ Colombia?   _____

5 _____ Oliver's father _____ Colombia?   _____

5 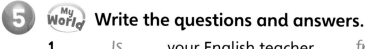 Write the questions and answers.

1 _Is_ your English teacher _from_ Russia?   _____

2 _Where_ is your English teacher _from_ ?   _____

3 _____ is your favorite singer _____ ?   _____

4 _____ is your favorite food _____ ?   _____

6 **Put the words in order. Then match.**

1   you / were / When / born?
    When were you born?   [b]

2   were / Where / born? / you
    _____   [ ]

3   Hana / was / born? / When
    _____   [ ]

4   born? / Where / she / was
    _____   [ ]

5   When / born? / were / Alex and Ani
    _____   [ ]

6   they / born? / were / Where
    _____   [ ]

a   They were born in Russia.
b   I was born on September 9th.
c   She was born in Mexico.
d   I was born in Italy.
e   They were born on February 21st.
f   She was born on November 18th.

7 **Read and complete the questions and answers.**

Name	Date of birth	Place of birth
Megan	April 1st, 2005	Colombia
Tom	July 23rd, 2006	the United Kingdom
Juan	December 7th, 2005	France

1   ___*When*___ was Tom ___*born*___ ? He ___*was born on*___ July 23*rd*_____ , 2006.
2   _____ was Megan _____ ? She _____ in Colombia.
3   _____ Tom _____ ? _____ in the United Kingdom.
4   _____ Juan _____ ? _____ in _____ .
5   _____ Megan _____ ? _____ .
6   _____ Juan _____ ? _____ .

8 (My World) **Answer the questions.**

1   Where is your family from?   *My family is from* _____
2   Are you from Italy?   _____
3   Where was your father born?   _____
4   When was your mother born?   _____

9 (Think) **Read the story again and number.**

☐	**a**	They want to take the World Quiz together. The first question is about Colombia.
☐	**b**	They go to the reading room to email Ruby's pen pal. But it isn't the reading room!
☐	**c**	Ruby can email her pen pal. Her pen pal is from Colombia.
1	**d**	Jack and Ruby are at the library. They see a quiz.

10 **Read and write *true* or *false*.**

1   Ruby thinks the quiz sounds fun.   *true*

2   Ruby and Jack don't know which city in Colombia has a flower festival. _____

3   Ruby's pen pal is from Russia.   _____

4   They want to email Jack's sister.   _____

5   They want to win the quiz.   _____

11 (My World) **What can you do to show the value: Try new things?**

1   *You can eat new foods.* _____

2   _____

3   _____

4   _____

5   _____

Story   Value   **7**

Skills: *Reading*

12 **Read Tim's email and circle the correct answers.**

Hi Luis,

How are you? My name's Tim. I was born on May 28th, 2006. I'm from the United Kingdom, but my father's from Spain.

We have fun festivals in Cambridge. The Strawberry Fair is in June. It's on Saturday the 6th. There are circus acts, music, and dance. In July, there's a big music festival called the Cambridge Folk Festival. The music is fantastic.

Where are you from in Spain? Do you know the festival called Tamborrada? It's in San Sebastian, Spain. People play music on drums. It sounds like fun. I'd like to go someday. Please write and tell me about Spain.

Your pen pal, Tim

Tamborrada, San Sebastian, Spain

Cambridge Folk Festival, Cambridge, UK

1 Where's Tim's father from?
   a Cambridge   **b** the United Kingdom   **c** Spain

2 When is the Strawberry Fair?
   a June 6th   **b** in Cambridge   **c** in the fall

3 Which festival is in July in Cambridge?
   a the Strawberry Fair   **b** the Folk Festival   **c** the Circus Festival

4 Where's the drum festival?
   a in the United Kingdom   **b** in San Sebastian, Spain   **c** in Cambridge

13 **(TIP)** **How to use capital letters.**

Use capital letters with:
names: *Tim, Luis*   towns and countries: *Cambridge, Spain*
festivals: *Cambridge Folk Festival*   days and months: *Saturday, May*

Read Tim's email again and circle all the capital letters. Then:

1 underline the names of people in red.
2 underline the towns and countries in blue.
3 draw boxes around the names of festivals in red.
4 draw boxes around the days and months in blue.

Skills: *Writing*

  Make notes about you and your town.

About Me.

Name: _____ Birthday: _____ Where I'm from: _____

About our town.

Name: _____ Country: _____

When to do and see things.

1 What: _____ 2 What: _____

  When: _____   When: _____

  What it's like: _____   What it's like: _____

3 What: _____ 4 Ask your pen pal a question.

  When: _____ _____

  What it's like: _____ _____

  Write an email about your town to a pen pal.

Dear _____ ,

_____

_____

_____

_____

_____

_____

_____

_____

Your pen pal,

(your name) _____

What are mosaics made of?

1 **Read and match the questions and answers.**

1 Where can we see mosaic art today? `d`

2 What are mosaics?

3 What are mosaic tiles made of?

4 What do artists use to put the tiles on cardboard?

a Pictures with many small tiles.

b Stones, ceramic, glass, paper.

c Glue.

d In places like train stations and shopping malls.

2 **Read and match. Then complete the sentences.**

1

1 This mosaic is made of a lot of paper tiles. It shows a head, eyes, and a ___mouth___ .

2 This mosaic is made of small, colored tiles. It shows a head and legs.
It's a _____ .

3 This mosaic is made of marble. The mosaic is on a floor. The mosaic pattern shows circles and _____ .

3 **Draw a mosaic for your home. Write three sentences about it.**

Evaluation

1 **Complete the questions and answers.**

Hector: I ^{1} _was_ ^{2} _born_ ^{3} _on_ October 10th, 2005.

Gloria: Wow! I ^{4}_____ ^{5}_____ ^{6}_____ October 10th, 2005, too.

Hector: We have the same ^{7}_____ !

Gloria: ^{8}_____ your friend Rosa ^{9}_____ Mexico, too?

Hector: No, she ^{10}_____ . She's ^{11}_____ the United States, but she ^{12}_____ ^{13}_____ in Colombia.

Hector: Where are you from, Gloria?

Gloria: I'm ^{14} _from_ the United Kingdom. But my grandmother's ^{15}_____ China. Where are you ^{16}_____ ?

Hector: I'm ^{17}_____ Mexico.

Gloria: ^{18}_____ was Rosa ^{19}_____ ?

Hector: She ^{20} _was_ ^{21}_____ ^{22}_____ October 10th, 2006.

2 **Complete the sentences about this unit.**

✔ = I can …   ✗ = I can't …

☐ **1** … name ten countries.

☐ **2** … ask and answer questions about where people are from.

☐ **3** … ask and answer questions about when people are born.

☐ **4** … try new things.

☐ **5** … plan and talk about a tour of festivals using *I'd like to go to …* .

6 My favorite part of this unit is _____ .

1 Family and pets

1 Read and circle the correct words.

1 My cousin is good at math and English. He's … .
  a (smart)   **b** sporty   **c** naughty

2 Jim's new puppy likes eating shoes. It's … .
  a talkative   **b** hardworking **c** naughty

3 Lena's parents always say hello. They're … .
  a friendly   **b** shy   **c** artistic

4 I'm good at making models and painting. I'm … .
  a artistic   **b** kind   **c** funny

5 Alex's brother doesn't like saying hello to me. He's … .
  a kind   **b** smart   **c** shy

6 My friend Bill makes me laugh. He's … .
  a sporty   **b** funny   **c** hardworking

7 My uncle tells lots of stories. He's … .
  a talkative   **b** hardworking **c** naughty

2 *Think* Read and complete the sentences. Then write the names.

    _____   _____   _____ *Penny* _____   _____

1 Penny always talks on the phone. She's _____ *talkative* _____ .

2 My cousin Mark is always mountain biking or bowling. He's _____ .

3 My uncle Arun is a businessman. He is always at his office. He likes working.
  He's _____ .

4 My aunt Jill works in a hospital. She gives people things. She's _____ .

> **My picture dictionary** Go to page 85: Write the new words.

3 Look at Lee's graph. Then circle the correct words.

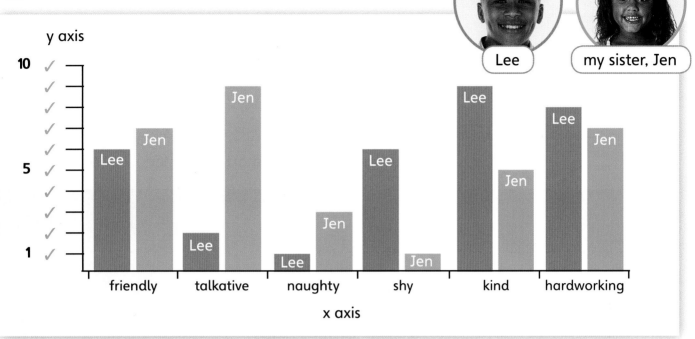

1 My sister, Jen, is **shyer** / **friendlier** than me.
2 I'm **more hardworking** / **naughtier** than my sister.
3 Jen is **kinder** / **more talkative** than me.
4 I'm **naughtier** / **kinder** than my sister.
5 My sister is **shyer** / **naughtier** than me.
6 I'm **shyer** / **more talkative** than my sister, Jen.

4 Look at activity 3. Complete the questions and answers.

1 Lee, is your sister ___naughtier than___ you? (naughty)   *Yes, she is.*

2 Lee, are you _____ your sister? (shy)   _____

3 Lee, are you _____ your sister? (talkative)   _____

4 Jen, is your brother _____ you? (kind)   _____

5 Jen, are you _____ your brother? (friendly)   _____

6 Jen, is your brother _____ you? (hardworking)   _____

5 Complete the questions and answers. Use the words in the box and your own ideas.

> sportier   more artistic   ~~shyer~~   more talkative

1 Are you _____*shyer*_____ than your friend?   _____

2 Are you _____ than your friend?   _____

3 Are you _____ than your friend?   _____

6 Complete the questions and answers with your own ideas.

1 ___Who's younger___ , your sister or your parrot? (young) My sister ___is younger___ .

2 _____ , you or your parrot? (old) My parrot _____ .

3 _____ , your cat or your dog? (quiet) My cat _____ .

4 _____ , your dog or your parrot? (noisy) My parrot _____ .

5 _____ , you or your sister? (tall) I _____ .

6 _____ , your sister or your father? (short) My sister _____ .

7 (My World) Write the questions and complete the answers. Then complete the chart.

1 (artistic / you / your mother)
   Who's more artistic, you or your mother?   I ___am___ .

2 (talkative / brother / sister)
   _____   My brother _____ .

3 (funny / your dog / your brother)
   _____   My dog _____ .

4 (quiet / your dog / your cat)
   _____   My cat _____ .

5 (tall / your father / your mother)
   _____   My father _____ .

artistic	quiet	hardworking	tall	sporty	talkative	funny
_me_		my mother		my sister		

8 (Think) **Read the story again. Match and then number.**

1	Jack and Ruby are __d__	**a**	answer the question.
	Sofia helps them ____	**b**	a message on a flower.
	Jack and Ruby read ____	**c**	than both of them today.
	They see Sofia. She is taller ____	**d**	at a flower festival.
	Sofia goes ____	**e**	with them.

9 **Read and circle the correct words.**

1 Jack and Ruby are in … .
  a Brazil **b** China **c** (Colombia)
2 Ruby thinks the message is from … .
  a her friend Sofia **b** the flowers **c** the festival
3 Sofia can help them … .
  a be taller **b** take the quiz **c** be very smart
4 Sofia is taller today because she's … .
  a in the festival **b** in Colombia **c** playing the game
5 The flower festival is in … .
  a London **b** Medellín **c** Mexico City

10 (My World) **What can you do to show the value: Learn about other cultures?**

1 You can visit other countries.

2 _____

3 _____

4 _____

5 _____

Story · Value **15**

Skills: *Reading*

11 Read and complete Camilla's report with the words in the box.
Then write the names under the pictures.

~~smart~~   funnier   naughty   quieter   talkative   older   naughtier

Our Pets, by Camilla

My family likes animals. I have a gray pet rabbit called Hugo.
He knows his name. I think he's ¹_____smart_____ .
He comes when I call him. But sometimes he's ²
_____ .   He eats the carrots in our garden!

My cousin Sam has a pet parrot. Her name is Paula. She's thirty-five
years old –   a lot ³_____ than Hugo.

Paula says things all the time. She's very ⁴_____ .
She's also ⁵_____ than my rabbit because she often
makes us laugh. My pet rabbit is a lot ⁶_____ than
Paula. Hugo doesn't say anything at all!

My brother also has a pet. It's a spider called Cob, and
I don't like it! Sometimes my brother puts it in my hat.
My brother's ⁷_____ than Hugo!

12 Look at activity 11. Answer the questions.

1   What does Hugo do that's naughty? _Hugo eats the carrots in Camilla's garden._
2   How old is Paula? _____
3   Who is funnier, Hugo or Paula? _____
4   Who is quieter, Hugo or Paula? _____
5   Who is naughtier, Hugo or Camilla's brother? _____

13 (TIP) **How to use *he*, *she*, and *it* for pets.**

Use *he* or *she* when you know the name of the pet:
Hugo is a boy rabbit. He's friendly.   Paula is a girl parrot. She's smart.

Use *it* when you don't know the name of the pet and when you don't know if the
animal is a boy or girl: *It's a spider called Cob, and I don't like it.*

Read Camilla's report again and circle *he*, *she*, and *it*.

Skills: *Writing*

  Make notes about two pets or animals you know.

Pet/Animal name:	What they're both like:	Pet/Animal name:
What it's like:	*friendly*	What it's like:

  Write a report about the two animals. Draw a picture.

Title: _____

How do **ant families** work together?

1 **Read and write *true* or *false*.**

1 A family of ants is called a colony. _____true_____

2 Ants work together in groups. _____

3 Families of ants live in rooms. _____

4 All ant colonies have three queens. _____

5 Some worker ants bring stones to the nest. _____

2 **How are the animals working together?**

1 a They are taking leaves to the nest.
  b They are cleaning the nest.
  c They are helping the queen ant.

2 a They are staying warm.
  b They are making a nest.
  c They are bringing food.

3 a They are looking for food for baby birds.
  b They are making a nest for baby birds.
  c They are watching the baby birds.

3 **Imagine that you are a worker ant. Write about your day and draw a picture.**

_____

_____

_____

_____

_____

_____

Evaluation

1 Put the words in order. Then match.

Robert

Gina

Sam

Olga

1 talkative / than / Robert, is / you? / Gina / more /

Robert, is Gina more talkative than you? [b]

2 than / Olga / taller / you? / Sam, is /

_____ [ ]

3 is / Gina? / you / or / Sam, who / quieter, /

_____ [ ]

4 Sam? / younger, Robert / or / Who is?

_____ [ ]

a is. / Sam /

_____

b No, / isn't. / she /

No, she isn't.

c is. / Gina /

_____

d is. / Yes, / she

_____

2 Look at activity 1 and complete the sentences. Use the words in the box.

1 Robert: I'm _____ _older_ _____ than Sam.

2 Gina is _____ than Olga.

3 Olga: I'm _____ than Gina.

4 Sam is _____ than Olga.

> artistic   ~~old~~
> short   sporty

3 Complete the sentences about this unit.

✔ = I can …   ✗ = I can't …

[ ] **1** … say ten new words about people.

[ ] **2** … talk about people using words like _smarter_ and _more hardworking than_.

[ ] **3** … ask and answer questions using _Who's older, you or your brother?_

[ ] **4** … learn about other cultures.

[ ] **5** … think and write about someone I know.

6 In this unit, I found _____ more interesting than

_____ .

2 On the playground

1 **Read and number the correct pictures. Then write.**

1   You can do this to play a game or talk
    to someone. _____use a cell phone_____

2   You can send a message to a friend
    this way. _____

3   You can do this in a baseball game.

    _____

4   This is noisier than talking.

    _____

5   You can do this when something is funny.

    _____

6   You do this in some sports, but it's not
    running or hopping. _____

2 **Think** **Read and circle the ones that don't belong.**

1   Things you do on the playground.
    a throw a ball   **b** (litter)   **c** skip   **d** laugh

2   Things you want to do with friends.
    a cry   **b** laugh   **c** text   **d** throw a ball

3   Things you can use a cell phone to do.
    a help others   **b** text friends   **c** laugh   **d** hop

4   Don't do these things in the house.
    a litter   **b** help others   **c** shout   **d** throw a ball

    My picture dictionary ➡ **Go to page 86: Write the new words.**

3 Complete the sentences with *should* or *shouldn't*.

1 You ___shouldn't___ use a cell phone on a bike.

2 You _____ stop at a green traffic light.

3 You _____ stop at a red traffic light.

4 You _____ use a cell phone in the movie theater.

5 You _____ litter on the beach.

6 You _____ put litter in the trash cans.

4 Read and write sentences with *should* or *shouldn't*.

1 We're at the movie theater. We get a text. We want to text our friend.

We ___shouldn't___ text in the movie theater.

2 We're on the street. We want to go to the shopping mall across from us. There is a crosswalk.

We _____ use the crosswalk.

3 We're at the museum. We see a painting. We want to touch it.

We _____ touch the painting.

4 We're at a shopping mall. We want to run and shout with our friend.

We _____ run and shout in the shopping mall.

5 After playing, we want to eat a sandwich.

We _____ wash our hands before we eat.

5 **My World** Write sentences using *should* or *shouldn't* and the phrases in the boxes.

> at home   in the classroom   ~~in the library~~   in the restaurant

1 _We should be quiet in the library._ .

2 _____ .

3 _____ .

4 _____ .

6 Put the words in order.

1 page, / Read / please. / this
Read this page, please.

2 cookies, / me / Give / the / please.

_____

3 please. / the / Anna / Pass / glue,

_____

4 me / Bring / cell phone, / please. / the

_____

5 photograph, / please. / Show / the class / your

_____

6 Read / please. / the / me / story,

_____

7 Read and write the numbers from activity 6.

1 **Jill:** I have a new book. It has a funny story.
  Amy: _____6_____

2 **Anna:** Oh, no! I need some glue.
  Teacher: _____
  Bill: Here you are, Anna.

3 **Mother:** I need to make a phone call. _____
  Mike: Here you are, Mom.

4 **Tom:** These cookies are nice.
  Father: You shouldn't eat cookies before dinner, Tom. _____

5 **Jim:** I have a photograph of my new baby brother.
  Teacher: _____

6 **Teacher:** OK, class. Open your books to page 43. _____

8 My World Use the words to write instructions.

1 *Bring me the eraser, please.* _____ (the eraser)

2 _____ (your photographs)

3 _____ (the cell phone)

4 _____ (your own idea)

9 (Think) **Read the story again. Then put the words in order and number.**

a shouldn't / the / The children / monkey. / feed

_____

b Sofia / wants / to / give / the / monkey / some / fruit.

1 _Sofia wants to give the monkey some fruit._____

c too. / is / Capu / in / school, / the

_____

d school. / hide / in / They / a

_____

10 **Read and complete. Use the words in the box.**

| ~~1850~~   can take   classroom   monkey   shouldn't   South America |

It's London, in ¹_____1850_____. The children do something they ²_____

do. A man is angry. They run and hide in a ³_____. Capu hides there, too.

Capu is a capuchin ⁴_____. He wants to go to ⁵_____.

The children ⁶_____ Capu home.

 11 **What can you do to show the value: Be kind to animals?**

1 _You can take the dog for a walk._____

2 _____

3 _____

4 _____

5 _____

Skills: *Reading*

 12 **Read and complete the letter with *should* or *shouldn't*.**

Jill can help!

Dear Jill,

I want to be an actor! I go to acting school. At my new school, my teacher says I'm too quiet. She says I
¹ __should__ talk more.

Sometimes we play a game. You throw a ball to a friend. They catch it and do something funny. Then they throw it to you, and you do something funnier. But I can't catch the ball, and my friends laugh at me.

I'm bad at acting.

Marina

Dear Marina,

You ² _____ worry!
It's really difficult to start a new school, but you ³ _____ be quiet and shy. You should be more talkative.

When you play the game, don't catch the ball. Drop it and do something funny. It's good to make your friends laugh. Or you
⁴ _____ learn to catch the ball and do something sporty. Or do both! An actor ⁵ _____ learn to do many things.

You should be hardworking, and you
⁶ _____ learn to act! Then you can have lots of fun.

Jill

13 **Look at activity 12. Read and match.**

1. Marina's teacher says she's quiet. `b`
2. Marina says she can't catch the ball. ☐
3. Marina says her friends laugh at her. ☐
4. Marina says she's bad at acting. ☐

a. Jill says it's good to be funny.
b. Jill says she shouldn't be shy.
c. Jill says she should drop the ball to be funny or learn to catch it.
d. Jill says she should be hardworking and learn to act.

 14 **(TIP)** **How to use *say/says*.**

My teacher: You should be hardworking!

My teacher says I should be hardworking.

My parents: You shouldn't be noisy.

My parents say I shouldn't be noisy.

Read Marina's letter again and circle the things her teacher says.

Skills: *Writing*

15 Read and check three problems you want to help with.

> Dear (your name) _____ ,
>
> I like my new sports school, but I'm not very good at sports.
>
> I want to be a basketball player. My teacher says ...
>
> ☐ I can't catch/throw a ball.   ☐ I don't play every day.
>
> ☐ I'm not sporty.   ☐ I don't work hard.
>
> ☐ I'm noisy in the classroom.   ☐ My friend is sportier than me.
>
> Please help,
>
> Jim

16 Write the three problems you checked in activity 15. Then make notes about help you can give.

1: _____	2: _____	3: _____

17 Write a help letter to Jim.

> Dear Jim,
>
> _____
>
> _____
>
> _____
>
> _____
>
> _____ ,
>
> _____
>
> (your name) _____

Where are the places on the map?

1 **Look and complete the sentences.**

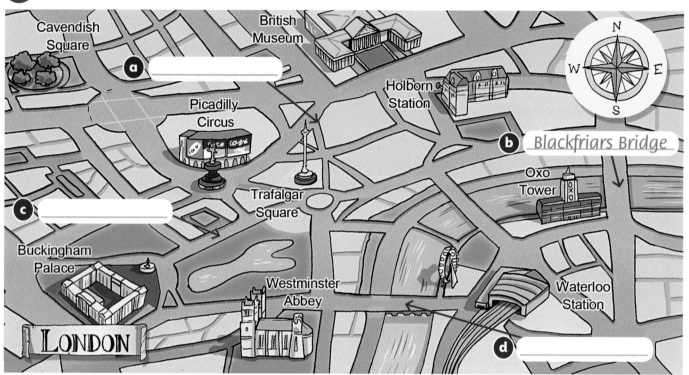

Cavendish Square
British Museum
Holborn Station
a _____
b _Blackfriars Bridge_
Picadilly Circus
Oxo Tower
c _____
Trafalgar Square
Buckingham Palace
Westminster Abbey
Waterloo Station
LONDON
d _____

N W E S

1 The _British Museum_ is in the north of the map.
2 South of Trafalgar Square is _____ .
3 You can see the Oxo Tower in the _____ of the map.
4 In the northwest of the map there's _____ Square.
5 Buckingham Palace is to the _____ of Westminster Abbey.

2 (Think) **Read and write the places in activity 1. Use the words in the box.**

~~Blackfriars Bridge~~   Monmouth Street   The Mall   Westminster Bridge

1 Blackfriars Bridge is to the east of the Oxo Tower.
2 Monmouth Street is to the south of the British Museum and to the north of Trafalgar Square.
3 The Mall is to the southwest of Trafalgar Square.
4 Westminster Bridge is to the west of Waterloo Station and to the southeast of Trafalgar Square.

Evaluation

1 **Read and correct the sentences.**

1 You ~~should~~ run in the house.
   _____shouldn't_____

2 We shouldn't listen to our teachers.
   _____

3 Tell me some paper, please.
   _____

4 Read me my cell phone, please.
   _____

5 We shouldn't be hardworking in class.
   _____

6 Pass us the answer, please.
   _____

2 **(My World)** **Write sentences about you.**

Write a rule for something you should do in school.

1 _I should_ _____

Write a rule for something you shouldn't do in school.

2 _____

Write an instruction for a friend.

3 _____

3 **Complete the sentences about this unit.**

✔ = I can ...   ✗ = I can't ...

☐ 1 ... use words like *skipping*, *texting*, *helping*.

☐ 2 ... talk about things we *should* and *shouldn't* do.

☐ 3 ... ask people to do things.

☐ 4 ... be kind to animals.

☐ 5 ... design and write about an unusual school and its rules.

6 The part of this unit I should practice is _____ .

Review Units 1 and 2

1 **Read and complete the sentences. Use the words in the box.**

> artistic   birthday   born   Brazil   smart   cry
> December   ~~funny~~   laugh   shout   sporty   throw

1 My best friend is very ___funny___ . She tells jokes. Her jokes make me _____ .

2 We shouldn't _____ or be noisy. We shouldn't make the baby _____ .

3 Will's _____ is on _____ 16th.

4 My younger brother is very _____ . He plays basketball. He can _____ the ball really far.

5 The new student is from _____ . But she was _____ in Spain.

6 My older sister is _____ . She paints and makes movies. Her movies always have a _____ story.

2 **Look and complete the sentences.**

1 I'm _more hardworking than_ my brother. (hardworking)

2 Your cat _____ your dog. (naughty)

3 _____ , John or his sister? (tall)

4 We _____ litter on the ground. (shouldn't/should)

3 Read and complete the sentences.

My name is Sam. There are three boys in my family. I was born on June 5th, 2006. I have two brothers. My brother Zack was born on May 4th, 2005. My other brother, Aiden, was born on July 6th, 2007.

Zack is tall and artistic. He's quiet and shy. He makes movies. Aiden is short. He's noisy and sporty. He plays soccer. I'm not short or tall. I'm friendly and talkative. I like playing video games on my cell phone.

| old/young |
| tall/short |
| noisy/quiet |

1 Zack is _____older_____ than me.
2 Aiden is _____ than me.
3 Zack is _____ than me.
4 Aiden is _____ than me.
5 I'm _____ than Aiden.
6 I'm _____ than Zack.

4 (Think) Who is Sam's mom talking to? Look at activity 3 and write the names and the words.

1 **Mom:** _____Aiden_____ ! You _____ kick the ball in the house.

_____ me the ball, please.

2 **Mom:** _____ ! You _____ use your cell phone during dinner.

3 **Mom:** _____ , _____ me your movie, please. I really want to watch it.

5 (My World) Answer the questions about you.

1 How many sisters or brothers do you have? How are you different from them?

I have _____

_____

2 What things are you good at?

_____

_____

3 What are the rules in your home? Use *should* and *shouldn't*.

_____

_____

3 Under the ocean

1 Look and write the words.

 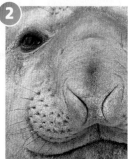 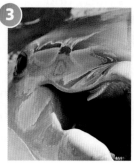  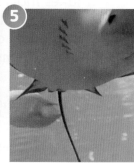

1 _____crab_____ 2 _____ 3 _____ 4 _____ 5 _____

2 Look, read, and write the words.

1 It has eight legs. It likes hiding in rocks. _____octopus_____

2 It has five legs. It can be many different colors. _____

3 It's a big fish. It has many sharp teeth. It's very dangerous! _____

4 It's very big. It's very heavy, too. It's not a fish. _____

5 It has a shell. It's good at swimming. _____

3 Think Complete the chart with the words in the box.

Which sea animals have … ?		
legs	a shell	a long tail
crab	crab	

crab
octopus
starfish
stingray
turtle
shark

My picture dictionary → Go to page 87: Write the new words.

4 **Read and complete the chart.**

dangerous	more dangerous	_the most dangerous_
heavy	heavier	
light	lighter	
intelligent	more intelligent	
strong	stronger	
weak	weaker	

5 **Complete the sentences. Use the words in parentheses.**

1 Stingrays aren't ___the most dangerous___ sea animals. (dangerous)

2 Blue whales are _____ whales. (heavy)

3 Seals aren't _____ sea animals. (weak)

4 Whale sharks are _____ sharks. (strong)

5 Turtles aren't _____ sea animals. (light)

6 Dolphins are _____ sea animals. (intelligent)

6 **Look and complete the sentences.**

heavy/light   fast/slow   dangerous/intelligent

1 The crab is ___the___ ___lightest___ .

2 The seal is _____ _____ .

3 The jellyfish is _____ _____ .

4 The dolphin is _____ _____ .

5 The dolphin is _____ _____ .

6 The shark is _____ _____ .

7 Read and complete. Use the words in the box.

~~heavy~~   intelligent   fast   slow   tall   small

Elephants are ¹ _the heaviest_ land animals. An elephant can weigh 7,000 kilograms. Elephants can be tall, too. But giraffes are ² _____ land animals. Giraffes can be 5.5 meters high. What about small land animals? Do you think a mouse or a bat is the smallest? ³ _____ land animals are bats. Bumblebee bats are only 30 mm long. ⁴ _____ land animals can run up to 120 kilometers per hour. They're large cats called cheetahs, and they live in Africa. ⁵ _____ land animals are turtles. They move at 0.27 kilometers per hour. Which land animals are ⁶ _____ ? Humans, of course, but chimpanzees are very intelligent, too.

8 (Think) Read and number the pictures.

elephant

chimpanzee

bumblebee bat

cheetah

1   It's not the strongest or the heaviest. It's not the smallest, and it's not the most intelligent. It's the fastest.
2   It's not the tallest or the fastest. It's not the most intelligent. It's the smallest.
3   It's not the smallest or the most intelligent. It's not the fastest. It's the strongest and the heaviest.
4   It's not the strongest or heaviest. It's not the fastest, and it's not the smallest. It's very intelligent.

9 (My World) Complete the questions and answers. Use the words in the box.

~~beautiful~~   friendly   interesting   dangerous

1   I think _____ are _the most beautiful_ sea animals.
2   I think _____ are _____ land animals.
3   Which sea animal is _____ ?
     I think _____ .
4   _____ animal is _____ ?
     I think _____ .

10 **Read the story again. Match and then number.**

☐	Capu finds _____	**a**	to cut the net.
1	Jack, Ruby, and Sofia are by _b_	**b**	the ocean.
☐	Jack uses the shell _____	**c**	is very friendly.
☐	The baby dolphin swims _____	**d**	a baby dolphin. It needs help.
☐	The dolphin's pod _____	**e**	to its pod.
☐	They see _____	**f**	the biggest shell.

11 **Read and complete. Use the words in the box.**

> help   pleasure   pod   trash   ~~Africa~~   thank you

Jack, Ruby, and Sofia are in ¹_____Africa_____ by the Indian Ocean. It's very beautiful. The children see something in the water. At first, it looks like ²_____ . But it's a baby dolphin.

They find shells, and they use them to ³_____ the dolphin. The dolphin swims with its ⁴_____ . The dolphin pod says ⁵_____ . It was a ⁶_____ for the children to help.

12   **What can you do to show the value: Keep our seas and oceans clean?**

1 Don't throw bottles in the ___ocean___ .

2 Don't make a _____ .

3 Clean up after a _____ .

4 Don't _____ .

Skills: *Reading*

13 **Read Sara's blog and circle the correct words.**

Sara's blog

Where **can** / **would** you like to go on vacation? How about a whale-watching trip in Alaska! You can **fly** / **go** to Alaska by car, plane, bus, or train. You can **have** / **sleep** in a hotel close to the ocean. Then you have to take a boat to go whale watching.

Whale watching is fun. You can **have** / **take** photographs. Here are some of my photographs. There were blue whales, brown seals, and beautiful jellyfish. But stay away from the jellyfish! They can **are** / **be** dangerous. My favorite sea animals are the dolphins. They're the most intelligent sea animals. They swim in groups called pods.

You should bring a warm coat and a hat when you go whale watching!

14 **Look at activity 13. Read and write *true* or *false*.**

1 You can go to Alaska by subway. _____*false*_____

2 You should take a boat to go whale watching. _____

3 Sara has photographs of blue starfish, brown crabs, and a friendly jellyfish. _____

4 Sara's favorite sea animals are octopuses. _____

5 You should bring warm clothes when you go whale watching. _____

15 **(TIP)** **How to use commas ,.**

When talking about two things, you don't need a comma:
I saw a dolphin and a whale.
When talking about more than two things, you do need a comma:
I saw a dolphin, a whale, a shark, a seal, <u>and</u> a starfish.
Write *and* before the last thing:
We took a plane, a bus, <u>and</u> a train.

Read Sara's blog again and:

1 circle the commas.

2 <u>underline</u> the sentence with two things that don't need a comma.

Skills: *Writing*

16   **Make notes about a place you want to go to.**

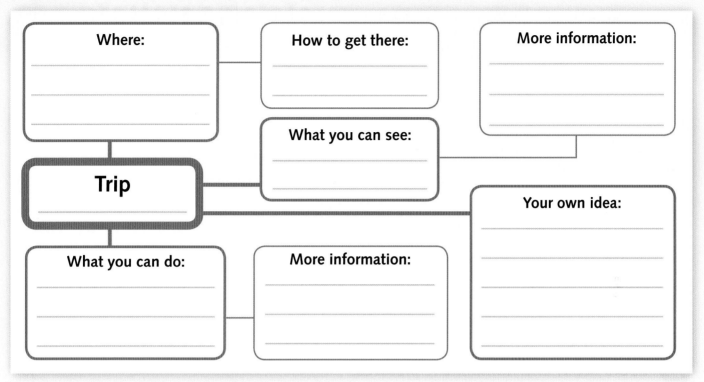

Where:

How to get there:

More information:

What you can see:

Trip

Your own idea:

What you can do:

More information:

17   **Write a blog and draw a picture.**

(Your name) _____'s blog

What is an **underwater** food chain?

1 **Read and complete the sentences.**

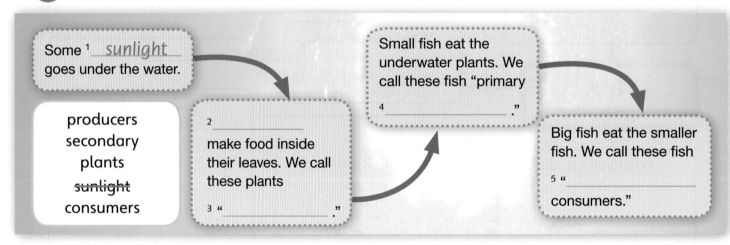

Some ¹ _sunlight_ goes under the water.

producers
secondary
plants
~~sunlight~~
consumers

² _____ make food inside their leaves. We call these plants

³ " _____ ."

Small fish eat the underwater plants. We call these fish "primary

⁴ _____ ."

Big fish eat the smaller fish. We call these fish

⁵ " _____ consumers."

2 **Look, read, and number the pictures.**

1 sunlight   **2** producer   **3** primary consumer   **4** secondary consumer

grass   snake   sunlight `1`   snail

butterfly   flowers   bird   sunlight

3 **Look at activity 2. Write the words.**

1 Snakes eat snails. Snakes are _secondary consumers_ .

2 Sunlight helps flowers make food. Flowers are _____ .

3 Snails eat grass. Snails are _____ .

4 Flowers and grass need _____ to make food.

Evaluation

1 **Read and complete.**

My name is Tina. I want to go scuba diving in the ocean.
I would like to swim with ¹_____turtles_____ . They are good
at swimming. And they are the oldest sea animals, too.

I wouldn't want to see any dangerous ²_____ .
They have a lot of teeth! And I would swim away from
the most dangerous sea animals, box ³_____ .

I would like to see ⁴_____ . They like to play
games.

⁵_____ are the biggest sea animals. And I think
whales are the most beautiful sea animals.

I would like to keep our oceans clean for all of the sea animals.

2 **Look at activity 1. Put the words in order and write the answers.**

1   are / oldest / sea animals? / Which / the
    Which are the oldest sea animals? _____   _____turtles_____

2   the / Which / most / sea animals? / are / dangerous
    _____   _____

3   the / biggest / sea animals? / are / Which
    _____   _____

4   think / most / beautiful / are the / sea animals? / Which / does / Tina
    _____

3 **Complete the sentences about this unit.**

✓ = I can …   ✗ = I can't …

☐ **1** … name ten sea animals.

☐ **2** … talk about animals using -*est* and *the most*.

☐ **3** … ask and answer questions using *Which … ?* and *the most*.

☐ **4** … keep our oceans clean.

☐ **5** … plan and talk about a weekend trip using *I'd like to*.

6   The part of this unit I found the most interesting is _____ .

4 Gadgets

1 Write the words.

1 m e g a s   n e s c o o l

    games console

2 b a l e t t

3 d o i v e   m a r e c a

4 s h e d o n h a p e

5 l i g t a d i   c a r e a m

6 P4M   r y l e p a

2 (Think) Read and complete the sentences.

1 He likes taking photographs. He doesn't have a camera. He uses his ___*smartphone*___ .

2 She likes playing games. She uses her _____ with the television.

3 He likes reading books. He doesn't have a tablet. He uses an _____ .

4 She does her homework on her _____ . It's bigger than her tablet, and she takes it to the library.

5 He watches movies on the _____ . It's bigger than his laptop.

3 (Think) Read and circle the ones that don't belong.

1 You can listen to music on … .
  a a laptop   **b** a smartphone   **c** an MP4 player   **d** (a video camera)

2 You can play games on … .
  a a digital camera   **b** a games console   **c** a tablet   **d** a laptop

3 You can read books on … .
  a a tablet   **b** headphones   **c** an e-reader   **d** a smartphone

4 You can use the Internet on … .
  a a tablet   **b** a laptop   **c** a video camera   **d** a smartphone

> **My picture dictionary** ➡ Go to page 88: Write the new words.

4 Complete the sentences about yesterday with words in the box.

listen to ~~play~~ study use ~~visit~~ watch

1 I _____visited_____ my grandmother.

2 We _____didn't play_____ tennis.

3 He _____ a smartphone to take photographs.

4 They _____ television in the evening.

5 She _____ music on her laptop.

6 You _____ English in the yard.

5 Read and correct the sentences.

1 They ~~visited~~ a movie last night before bed. ___watched___

2 I didn't play for my science test yesterday evening. _____

3 I listened movies on a tablet last weekend. _____

4 We studied games on our smartphones this morning before school. _____

5 He didn't watch to music on his MP4 player last night. _____

6 She used her grandmother last Saturday. _____

6 **My World** Write about last week. Use the words in the box and your own ideas.

1 Last weekend I _____ studied English. _____

2 Last week I didn't _____

3 _____

4 _____

use
~~study~~
watch
play

7 **Read and complete the questions and answers.**

Dear Sheila,
Thank you for the birthday present! It's great! I'm sorry you missed my birthday party last Saturday. It was fun. We played on my new games console. I took my dog for a walk in the park on Sunday.
How is your trip to Paris? Tell me about it! Send photographs!
Take care, Rian

Dear Rian,
I'm glad you like the hat. Sorry I missed your party. Paris is wonderful. I visited my cousins on Saturday. They don't speak English, but we played on a games console. On Sunday, we looked at paintings in the Louvre Museum and shopped on a street called the Champs-Élysées.
See you soon, Sheila

1 What _____*did*_____ Rian _____*do*_____ at her party?

She _*played on a games console*_ .

2 What _____ Rian _____ last Sunday?

She _____ in the park.

3 What _____ Sheila _____ with her cousins last Saturday?

They _____ .

4 _____ Sheila _____ last Sunday?

She _____ at paintings in the Louvre Museum and _____ on a street called the Champs-Élysées.

8 **(My World)** **Complete the questions and answers. Use your own information.**

1 What did you do last night? _*Last night, I watched TV.*_ _____

2 What didn't you do last night? _____

3 What did you do last Saturday? _____

4 What did you do yesterday after school? _____

9 (Think) **Read the story again and complete the sentences. Then number.**

	a	They find a _____ from 1950.
	b	The explorers think the _____ is a wonderful gadget.
	c	They should help the _____ .
1	**d**	The children are in _Antarctica_ . It's cold.
	e	Then they use the tablet to ask for _____ .

Antarctica
diary
tablet
help
explorers

10 **Read and match.**

1 There aren't any ___b___
2 The explorers are very _____
3 The children use blankets _____
4 A helicopter takes _____
5 The explorers say "thanks" _____

a cold, and they need help.
b trees in Antarctica.
c to the children.
d to help the explorers.
e the explorers to hospital.

11 (My World) **Write the sentences. Then check the ones that show the value: Use technology wisely.**

1 laptop / to / can / You / a / use / do homework.
  You can use a laptop to do homework. ☑

2 study English. / a tablet / use / You / can / to
  _____ ☐

3 play / can / in / You / a / games console / on / class.
  _____ ☐

4 to ask / use / cell phone / You / for help. / a / can
  _____ ☐

Story   Value   **41**

Skills: *Reading*

 12 **Read Ben's report and circle the correct answers.**

Inventions, by Ben

GRIDpad tablet

Television

Samsung invented the first tablet in 1989. They called it the GRIDpad. It was bigger and heavier than the tablets we have today. You used a pen with it!

Then Jeff Hawkins invented a smaller tablet called the Palm Pilot in 1996. It used the GRIDpad's pen. The Palm Pilot was really cool!

John Logie Baird didn't invent the television. Many people worked together to invent the television. But Baird showed the first television pictures to people. The first television pictures were black and white. Baird showed the first color pictures to people on July 3, 1928. The first television used a telephone to send pictures!

1 Which gadget was invented in 1989?
   a the laptop b the television c the tablet
2 How was the first tablet different from today's tablets?
   a It was bigger and heavier. b It was smaller and lighter.
   c It was bigger and lighter.
3 Who showed the first television pictures to people?
   a Jeff Hawkins b John Logie Baird c many people
4 What did people see on July 3, 1928?
   a pictures on black and white television b pictures on color television
   c pictures on a tablet
5 Which gadget was invented first?
   a the Palm Pilot b the television c the GRIDpad

 13 **TIP** **How to use periods ( ) and exclamation points ( ).**

Usually you use a period to end a sentence: *It's an old laptop.*

You can use an exclamation point when you want to: shout – *Hey! Wow!*
make sentences stronger and more exciting – *It's great! Thanks!*

Read Ben's report again and circle the exclamation points.

Skills: *Writing*

14 Find out about a gadget or other invention. Make notes about it.

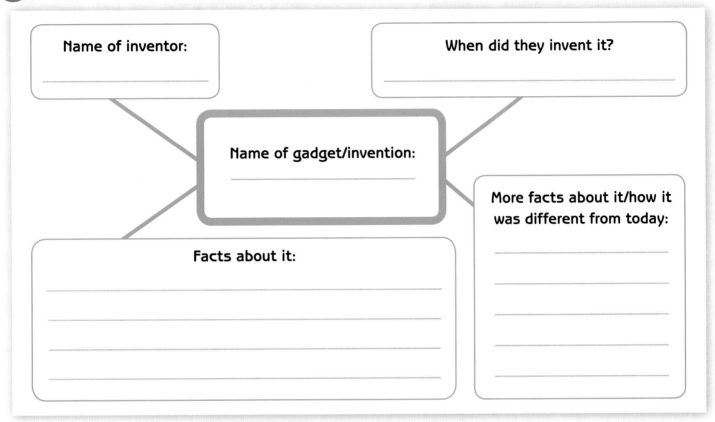

Name of inventor:
_____

When did they invent it?
_____

Name of gadget/invention:
_____

More facts about it/how it
was different from today:
_____
_____
_____
_____
_____

Facts about it:
_____
_____
_____
_____

15 Write a report about the gadget or invention.

Title: _____
_____
_____
_____
_____
_____
_____
_____
_____
_____
_____

1 How many computer games did the class buy last year?
Draw the data on the line chart.

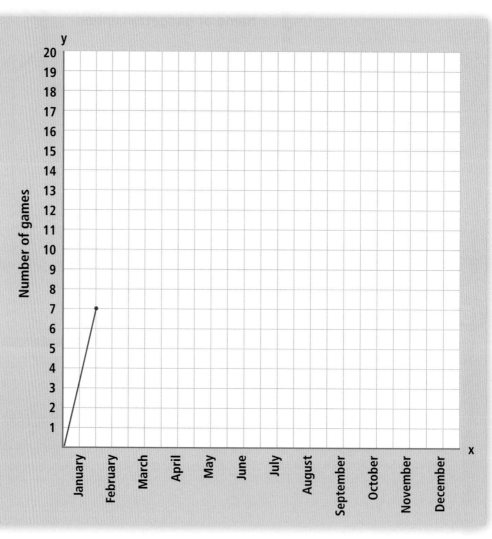

Month	Number of computer games
January	7
February	3
March	10
April	12
May	9
June	6
July	16
August	18
September	4
October	7
November	5
December	20

2 Look at activity 1. Answer the questions.

1 What data is on the x-axis? _____ *the months* _____

2 What data is on the y-axis? _____

3 Which month shows the peak for buying computer games? _____

4 When is the biggest rise in buying computer games? _____

5 When is the biggest fall in buying computer games? _____

Evaluation

1 **Read the conversation and correct the eight mistakes.**

Dana: What do you do last weekend, Brice?

Brice: I play on my games console. Then I watch a soccer game on television. What did you do?

Dana: I study on my e-reader. Then I listen to music on my new MP4 player. What did you do, Helen?

Helen: I use my smartphone to make a video.

Dana: Can we watch it?

Helen: Sure. Here it is. I use my laptop to add music to the video.

Dana: That's great!

Brice: Tom, what did you do last weekend?

Dana: Hey! Look! Is that Tom in the video?

Tom: Yes, that's me. I help Helen make her video!

1 _____did_____   2 _____   3 _____   4 _____

5 _____   6 _____   7 _____   8 _____

2 **Look at activity 1. Complete the questions and answers.**

1 What ___did___ Brice ___do___ last weekend?

He _played on his games console_ and _watched a soccer game on television_ .

2 What _____ Dana _____ last weekend?

She _____ . Then she _____ .

3 Which gadgets _____ Helen use last weekend?

She used her _____ and her _____ to make a video.

4 What _____ Tom _____ last weekend? He _____ .

3 **Complete the sentences about this unit.**

✔ = I can …   ✗ = I can't …

☐ 1 … name ten gadgets.

☐ 2 … say what I did last weekend using *watched*, *listened*, *played*, *used*, *visited*, and *studied*.

☐ 3 … ask and answer questions using *What did you do … ?*

☐ 4 … use technology wisely.

☐ 5 … think and write about my favorite gadget.

6 The part of this unit I found the most useful is _____ .

Review Units 3 and 4

1 Look and complete the word puzzle.

Across

Down

2 Read and complete the sentences.

1 You wear ___headphones___ on your head to listen to music.

2 A _____ is a computer. It's smaller than a laptop and bigger than a smartphone.

3 You keep your music on an _____ . You can't make phone calls or watch movies on it. But you can use it to listen to music.

4 I like to read books on my _____ . I can only use it to read books.

5 My _____ is smaller than my laptop, and it does more things. I can use it as an MP4 player, as a video camera, and to talk to my friends!

6 My favorite technology is my _____ . I really like video games.

3 Look and complete the questions and answers. Then match.

1 What _did_ _you_ _do_ in the park last weekend? [c]

2 _____ sea animal is the most intelligent? [ ]

3 _____ bird is the strongest? [ ]

4 What _____ you watch on television last night? [ ]

a The dolphin is the _____ intelligent.

b I _____ a program about sharks on television.

c I ___played__ soccer with my friends.

d The eagle is the _____ bird.

4 (Think) Read and complete the sentences.

Abby watched a TV program about the heaviest sea animal last night.

Alan and Tina played a game about the strongest sea animal on their smartphones.

Tom took a quiz on his tablet last night. He learned about the most dangerous sea animal.

Rose used her laptop last night. She looked at pictures of the most dangerous fish.

1 Rose _didn't_ _play_ on her smartphone. She _looked_ _at_ _pictures_ of ____sharks____ .

2 _____ and _____ played a game on their _____ .

3 _____ , _____ , and _____ looked at whales last night.

But they _____ the same gadgets.

4 Tom _____ about box _____ .

5 Abby didn't use a laptop or smartphone last night. She _____ television.

5 (My World) Answer the questions about you.

1 What are your favorite sea animals? _My favorite sea animals are_ _____

2 What did you do last weekend? _____

3 What didn't you do last weekend? _____

4 Which gadget is your favorite? _____

The natural world

1 **Read and circle the correct words.**

1   You can climb a … . It's tall.
   a mountain   **b** forest   **c** jungle

2   A … is like a mountain. It's very hot and dangerous.
   a mountain   **b** island   **c** volcano

3   You find this land in an ocean or a lake. You can go to an … by boat.
   a island   **b** cave   **c** lake

4   A … is smaller than the ocean. People go sailing on it.
   a lake   **b** island   **c** river

5   A … is water that moves across land. The Amazon is the name of one.
   a desert   **b** lake   **c** river

6   The Amazon is also the name of a … . It's hot and has a lot of trees.
   a mountain   **b** jungle   **c** desert

7   There are many trees in a … . It can be cold or hot.
   a lake   **b** volcano   **c** forest

8   It's very hot and there is sand in the … .
   a volcano   **b** desert   **c** waterfall

9   A … is under the ground or in a mountain. Bats sometimes live in it.
   a desert   **b** waterfall   **c** cave

10   Water that falls from a mountain or higher land is a … .
   a waterfall   **b** lake   **c** island

2 **Write the sentences.**

1   (island / small / ocean)

   An island is smaller than an ocean.

2   (mountain / tall / tree)

   _____

3   (forest / cool / jungle)

   Usually, _____

4   (desert / dry / jungle)

   _____

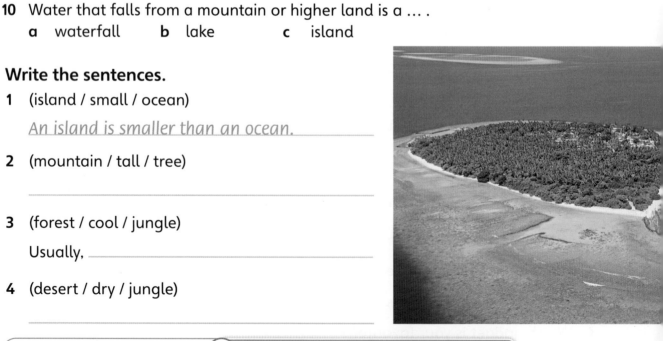

My picture dictionary **Go to page 89: Write the new words.**

3 **Read Dave's and Amber's vacation lists. Correct the mistakes in the sentences.**

Dave's vacation
- [ ] swim in the lake
- [✓] catch fish
- [✓] go to the forest
- [ ] see a deer
- [✓] eat fish
- [ ] eat pizza
- [✓] drink juice

Amber's vacation
- [✓] go skiing
- [ ] go snowboarding
- [✓] drink juice
- [✓] eat chocolate
- [ ] eat pizza
- [✓] have a party
- [✓] swim at the hotel

1 Dave and Amber ~~drink~~ juice on their vacations. _____drank_____

2 Dave don't swim in a lake on his vacation. _____
Amber swim at the hotel. _____

3 Dave eat fish. Amber eat chocolate. _____

4 Amber don't go snowboarding. She go skiing. _____

5 Dave don't have a party. Amber don't go to the forest. _____

4 **Look at activity 3. Read and complete the answers.**

1 Where did Dave go?   Dave _went to the forest_ _____ .
2 What didn't Dave see?   Dave _____ .
3 What did Dave catch?   He _____ .
4 What did Amber have?   Amber _____ .
5 What didn't Amber or Dave eat?   They _____ .

5 **(My World) Answer the questions about you.**

1 Where did you go on your favorite vacation?

On my favorite vacation, I went to _____

2 What did you do on your favorite vacation?

_____

3 What didn't you do on your favorite vacation?

_____

4 What did you eat on your favorite vacation?

_____

6 (Think) **Complete the questions and answers.**

Mom: ¹ __Did__ you ² __go__ on a trip this afternoon?

Mel: Yes, I ³ __did__ . My class ⁴_____ on a trip.

Mom: ⁵_____ you swim in a lake?

Mel: No, I ⁶_____ .

Mom: ⁷_____ you see a painting?

Mel: No, I ⁸_____ . I saw a cow.

Mom: A cow? ⁹_____ you ¹⁰_____ horses?

Mel: Yes, I ¹¹_____ . I saw horses, cows, and bees.

Mom: That's nice. ¹²_____ you ¹³_____ milk?

Mel: Yes, I ¹⁴_____ . I drank milk from the cows. I ate apples from the trees, too.

Mom: Hmm, apples, cows ... I know! ¹⁵_____ you visit a ¹⁶_____ ?

Mel: Yes, I did!

7 (My World) **Complete the questions and answers about you.**

1 __Did__ you __drink__ coffee yesterday?

_____

2 _____ your family _____ a museum yesterday?

_____

3 _____ your friend _____ to school yesterday?

_____

4 _____ your friend _____ in a lake yesterday?

_____

8 (Think) **Read the story again. Then put the words in order and number.**

a   can't / he / Jack / thinks / act. /

   [ ] _____

b   doesn't / bats. / Sofia / like

   [ ] _____

c   the / The / director / thanks / children.

   [ ] _____

d   a / are / children / cave. / in / The

   [1] *The children are in a cave.*

e   The / children / director / the / needs / to help.

   [ ] _____

9 **Read and circle the correct words.**

1   Ruby doesn't like … .
   a   acting   b (bats)   c   the dark

2   There are … in the cave.
   a   actors   b   bats   c   a director

3   They can help because the director needs … .
   a   doesn't worry   b   actors   c   is in the United States

4   Jack worries about … .
   a   acting   b   dogs   c   the dark

5   Hollywood is … .
   a   a movie   b   where they take Capu   c   in the United States

10 (My World) **Write the sentences. Then check the ones that show the value: Encourage your friends.**

1   can / You / it! / do
   You can do it! [✓]

2   aren't / good at / You / sports!
   _____ [ ]

3   actor! / a / You're / great
   _____ [ ]

4   We / can / you! / help
   _____ [ ]

5   cooking! / You / good at / aren't
   _____ [ ]

Skills: *Reading*

11 Read the vacation reviews. Change the <u>underlined</u> words to say what happened. Then match.

VACATION HIKES REVIEWS

1 Amazon River jungle trip, by Amy

I ¹<u>go</u> on the Amazon River jungle trip in July. That was a good time to go because it wasn't rainy. I ²<u>go</u> on a boat trip down the long river. I didn't swim in the river because I ³<u>see</u> a big snake in the water. We ⁴<u>eat</u> lots of delicious bananas on this trip. My favorite part of the trip? I ⁵<u>see</u> a monkey and a jaguar!

2 Grand Canyon horse ride, by Jim

I ⁶<u>see</u> so many things in the Grand Canyon! It's not just rocks and sand. Our guide pointed to lots of green lizards, pretty birds, and beautiful flowers! We ⁷<u>go</u> on horses. But sometimes the naughty horses wouldn't walk! We ⁸<u>eat</u> cookies and ⁹<u>drink</u> water. At night, it was very dark. We ¹⁰<u>see</u> so many stars. It was beautiful.

1 ___went___	2 _____	3 _____	4 _____
5 _____	6 _____	7 _____	8 _____
9 _____	10 _____		

12 Look at activity 11. Answer the questions.

1 Does it rain in July in the Amazon?   No, it doesn't.
2 What was Amy's favorite part of her trip? _____
3 What animals can you see in the Grand Canyon? _____
4 What were the horses like? _____

13 **(TIP)** How to describe things.

Use lots of different words to make your reviews more interesting:
I went down a *long* river.
I saw *green* lizards, pretty birds, and *beautiful* flowers.
Read the vacation reviews again and:

1 circle three examples of words that describe things in Amy's review.
2 circle five examples of words that describe things in Jim's review.

Skills: *Writing*

14   **Make notes about a place you visited. Use words to describe things.**

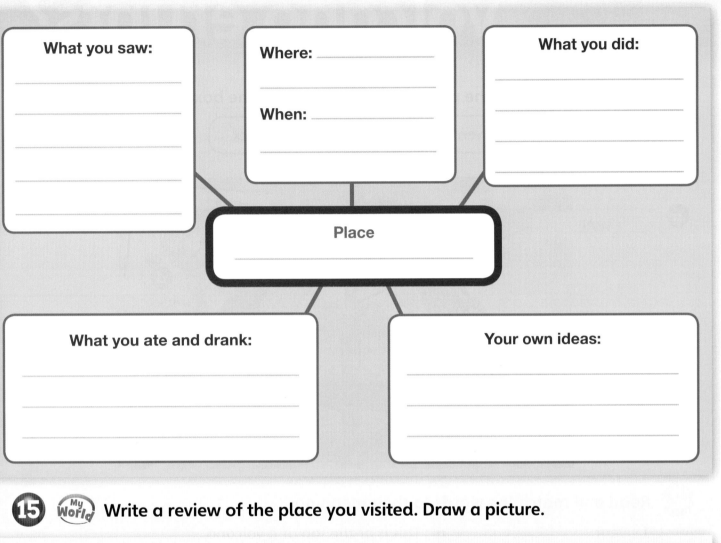

What you saw:

Where: _____

When: _____

What you did:

Place

What you ate and drank:

Your own ideas:

15 **Write a review of the place you visited. Draw a picture.**

What happens when a volcano erupts?

1 Look and complete the picture with the words in the box.

vent   crater   lava   ash   rock

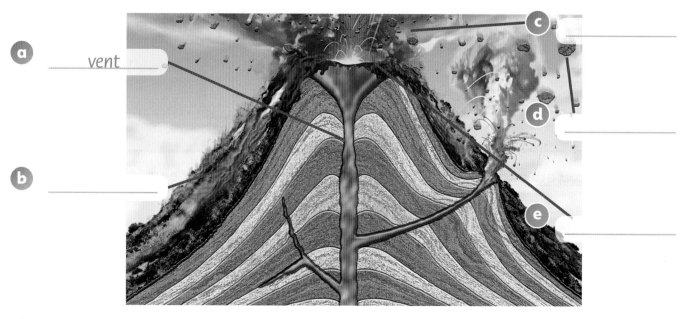

a _____ vent _____

b _____

c _____

d _____

e _____

2 Read and match the words to their meanings.

1 vent — c
2 crater — [ ]
3 lava — [ ]
4 ash and rocks — [ ]
5 plants — [ ]

a This is at the top of a volcano.
b Hot lava can stop these from growing.
c This is inside a volcano. Very hot material comes up it.
d This very hot material comes from inside the volcano.
e These fly into the air above the erupting volcano.

3 Think Read and complete the sentences. Then number.

[ ] a The lava cools and turns to _____ .

[ ] b Lava covers the _____ , and they stop growing.

[1] c You can see _____ rocks _____ and _____ in the air.

[ ] d _____ runs down the sides of the volcano.

plants
ash
rock
rocks
lava

Evaluation

1 **Complete the questions and answers.**

1 Erin: I ¹_____went_____ somewhere interesting this weekend.

   Jack: ²_____Did_____ you ³_____see_____ any birds?

   Erin: No, I didn't, but I ⁴_____ bats!

   Jack: Let me guess. Was it dark?

   Erin: Yes!

   Jack: You ⁵_____ to a ⁶_____ .

2 Dan: Mike, guess where I ⁷_____ on vacation!

   Mike: ⁸_____ you ⁹_____ lots of trees?

   Dan: Yes, ¹⁰_____ , but we didn't climb them.

   Mike: ¹¹_____ you ¹²_____ hot chocolate?

   Dan: Yes, ¹³_____ .

   Mike: ¹⁴_____ you ¹⁵_____ snowboarding or skiing?

   Dan: Yes, ¹⁶_____ .

   Mike: I know! You ¹⁷_____ to the ¹⁸_____ !

2 **Look at activity 1. Answer the questions.**

1 Did Erin see any birds on vacation?   _No, she didn't._

2 Did Erin go to a dark place?   _____

3 Did Dan climb any trees?   _____

4 Did Dan drink hot chocolate?   _____

3 **Complete the sentences about this unit.**

✓ = I can …   ✗ = I can't …

☐ 1 … name ten places in the natural world.

☐ 2 … say what I did in my vacation using *had*, *went*, *saw*, *swam*, *ate*, *drank*, and *caught*.

☐ 3 … ask and answer *yes* and *no* questions using *Did you … ?*

☐ 4 … encourage my friends.

☐ 5 … think and write about my favorite vacation.

6 The part of this unit I enjoyed the most was _____ .

6 Helping at home

1 Read and complete the sentences.

Every morning, I get up.
Then I ___make my bed___ .

We _____
every week.

Every day, my mom
_____ .

My sister usually
_____ .

Sometimes I help my mom
_____ .

I play soccer, and then I
_____ .

2 Complete the chart.

Things you do in the kitchen	Things you do in the bedroom	Things you do in many rooms
dry the dishes	_____	_____
_____	_____	_____

3 (Think) Circle the ones that don't belong.

1 Clean the ... .
   a basement   b (soccer)   c living room   d desk
2 Dry ... .
   a your clothes   b your hair   c a headache   d the dishes
3 Clean the ... .
   a boat   b car   c bike   d talkative
4 Sweep the ... .
   a floor   b garage   c stairs   d sunny

My picture dictionary → Go to page 90: Write the new words.

4 Read and circle the correct words.

Hi Kayla,

Do you ¹**have to** /don't have to help at home? We do! First, my older sister ²**has to** / doesn't have to make breakfast. Then, I ³**have to** / don't have to wash the dishes and dry them. But I ⁴**have to** / don't have to sweep the floor. My sister has to do that. And I'm happy I ⁵**have to** / don't have to take the trash out. My younger brother ⁶**has to** / doesn't have to do that. Write back soon!

Your friend, Jackie

Hi Jackie,

You're busy! My parents do everything, so I usually ⁷**have to** / don't have to help at my house. This week is different. I ⁸**have to** / don't have to help around my grandmother's house. I ⁹**have to** / don't have to wash clothes for her. Then I ¹⁰**have to** / don't have to clean the living room. I ¹¹**have to** / don't have to cook dinner for her. My brother does that. What do you have to do this weekend? Can we go to the movies?

Your friend, Kayla

5 Look at activity 4. Write the questions and answers.

1 (Jackie / make breakfast)

   Does Jackie have to make breakfast?   *No, she doesn't.*

2 (Jackie / wash and dry dishes)

   _____   _____

3 (Jackie's sister / sweep the floor)

   _____   _____

4 (Jackie / take the trash out)

   _____   _____

5 (Kayla / clean the living room / this week)

   _____   _____

6 (Kayla's mother / cook dinner / this week)

   _____   _____

6 Put the words in order. Then match to the correct answers.

1 you / have / Monday? / on / to / What / do / do

What do you have to do on Monday? **b**

a They have to wash the car.

2 What / on / John / do / have / to / Monday? / does

_____ ☐

b I have to clean my bedroom.

3 on / Tuesday? / do / have / does / Poppy / What / to

_____ ☐

c Ethan does.

4 has / the / Who / on / wash / to / Tuesday? / car

_____ ☐

d He has to take the trash out.

5 Tina and Rob / do / What / have / to / do / on / Tuesday?

_____ ☐

e She has to clean the kitchen.

7 (Think) Look at activity 6. Write the names in the chart.

	Monday	Tuesday
clean the kitchen	Tina and Rob	
take the trash out		me
clean my bedroom	me	John
wash the car	Poppy	

8 (My World) Complete the questions and answers about you.

1 What do you have to do on Monday?

On Monday, I have to _____

2 What do you have to do in English class?

_____

3 Who has to go to school?

_____

4 What does your friend have to do tomorrow?

_____

5 Who has to do homework?

_____

9 Look, read, and write *true* or *false*.

Picture 1

1   The children are helping the people.   _true_

2   Capu is watering the plants.   _____

3   Sofia is sweeping the stairs.   _____

4   Ruby is painting the palace.   _____

Picture 2

5   Capu wants to help the man.   _____

6   Capu can't find the key.   _____

10 (Think) Read the story again. Match and then number.

□	Capu finds _____		**a**	the workers finish the palace.
□	The workers have to _____		**b**	the key on the worker.
1	The children are at a palace _d_		**c**	finish the palace.
□	The worker can't _____		**d**	in ancient Egypt.
□	The children help _____		**e**	find the key to the palace.

11 (My World) What can you do to show the value: Help other people?

1   _You can dry the dishes._

2   _____

3   _____

4   _____

5   _____

Skills: *Reading*

12 **Read and complete the postcards with *have to* or *don't have to*.**

Dear Alex,

I live at my grandpa's house now. He has lots of pets! We
¹ <u>have to</u> wake up early every day. Then we feed the
dogs, cats, and fish. On Saturday, I ² _____ wash the
rabbits. They are my favorite animals! We ³ _____ buy
any fruit because grandpa grows it in his garden! Grandpa's fruit
is really good! We ⁴ _____ help him in the yard after
school.

Do you like living on a houseboat?

Write to me soon!
Lola

Dear Lola,

Thanks for your postcard! My family's houseboat is small! We
⁵ _____ be very clean. We ⁶ _____ buy food often
because we grow vegetables on the boat. We also share a garden on the
land.

There is a bird's nest on the roof. We ⁷ _____ feed the birds
because they eat fish from the river.

Come and visit and see the seals! They're always close to the boat!
Alex

13 **Look at activity 12. Answer the questions.**

1 What does Lola do in the morning? <u>She feeds the dogs, cats, and fish.</u>

2 Who buys fruits more often? Lola or Alex? _____

3 What does Lola do after school? _____

4 What two animals can Alex see? _____

5 What does Alex want Lola to do? _____

14 **How to use apostrophes().**

We use apostrophes to show that a person or thing has something.

The family's car ... = the car that the family has
The dog's toy = the toy that the dog has

Read the letters again and circle the apostrophes that show that people or animals have something.

Skills: *Writing*

15 **Circle *at home* or *in school*. Make notes about things you *have to / don't have to* do.**

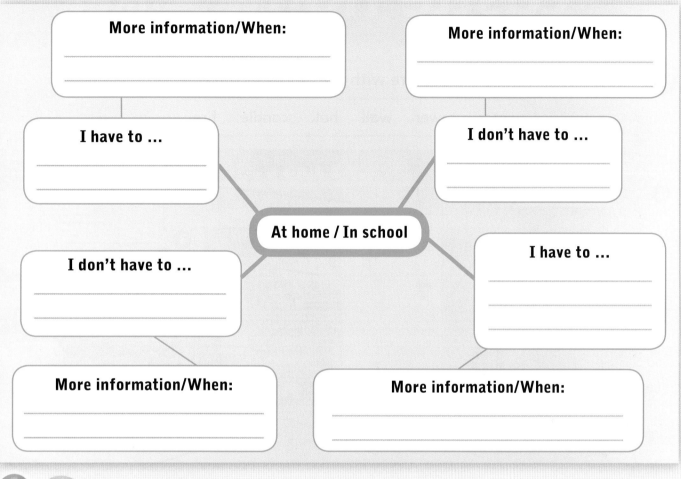

More information/When:
_____
_____

More information/When:
_____
_____

I have to …
_____
_____

I don't have to …
_____
_____

At home / In school

I don't have to …
_____
_____

I have to …
_____
_____
_____

More information/When:
_____
_____

More information/When:
_____
_____

16 **Write a postcard to a friend about what you *have to / don't have to* do.**

Dear _____ ,
_____
_____
_____
_____
_____
_____
_____
_____
(your name) _____

What were castle homes like?

1 **Look and complete the picture with the words in the box.**

water   tower   ~~wall~~   hall   candle   fire

1 _____wall_____

2 _____

3 _____

4 _____

5 _____

6 _____

2 **Read and complete.**

In the Middle Ages, there was ¹_____water_____ around most castles. There were also
big strong ²_____ . They had tall ³_____ in them. Inside castles,
families had meals around a long wooden ⁴_____ in the hall. People used
⁵_____ to see at night. The castles had a ⁶_____ for cooking food
on a big fire. Outside, there was a garden with fruits and ⁷_____ to eat.

3 **Imagine you go to a castle in the Middle Ages and meet a child there. Write
three questions for the child about life in the castle.**

1 _Do you have to_ _____ ?

2 _____ ?

3 _____ ?

Evaluation

1 Look and write what each person *has to / doesn't have to* do.

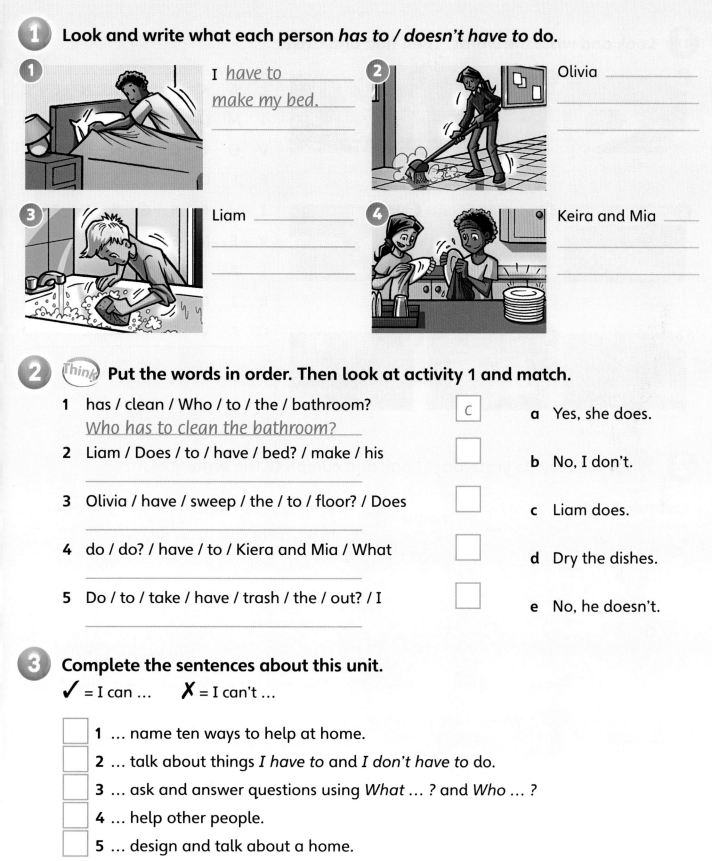

1 I *have to make my bed.*

2 Olivia _____

3 Liam _____

4 Keira and Mia _____

2 (Think) **Put the words in order. Then look at activity 1 and match.**

1 has / clean / Who / to / the / bathroom?
Who has to clean the bathroom? [c]

2 Liam / Does / to / have / bed? / make / his
_____

3 Olivia / have / sweep / the / to / floor? / Does
_____

4 do / do? / have / to / Kiera and Mia / What
_____

5 Do / to / take / have / trash / the / out? / I
_____

a Yes, she does.

b No, I don't.

c Liam does.

d Dry the dishes.

e No, he doesn't.

3 **Complete the sentences about this unit.**

✓ = I can …   ✗ = I can't …

[ ] **1** … name ten ways to help at home.

[ ] **2** … talk about things *I have to* and *I don't have to* do.

[ ] **3** … ask and answer questions using *What … ?* and *Who … ?*

[ ] **4** … help other people.

[ ] **5** … design and talk about a home.

6 The part of this unit I have to practice is _____ .

Review Units 5 and 6

1 Look and write the words. Then find and circle.

① island	②	③
④	⑤	⑥
⑦	⑧	⑨

L	A	K	E	R	F	N	L	L
I	M	O	U	N	T	A	I	N
V	O	L	C	A	N	O	R	I
R	F	O	R	E	S	T	D	I
I	V	F	R	G	E	R	E	S
V	E	N	E	I	A	F	S	L
E	A	E	T	E	A	J	E	A
R	J	U	N	G	L	E	R	N
C	A	V	E	R	A	E	T	D

2 What did they do yesterday? Look and complete the sentences.

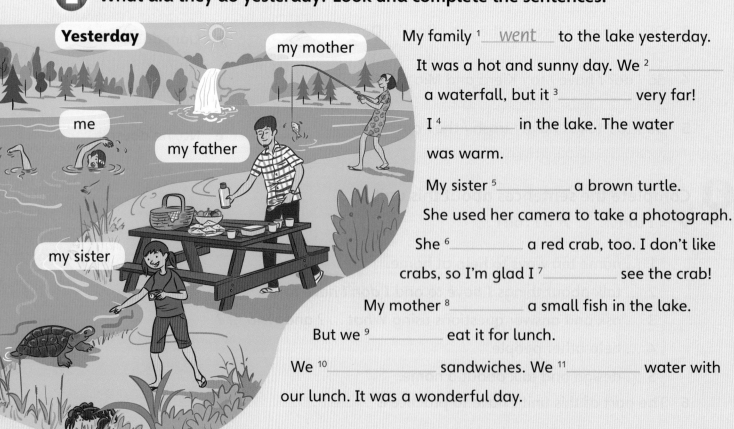

Yesterday
my mother
me
my father
my sister

My family ¹ _went_ to the lake yesterday.
It was a hot and sunny day. We ² _____
a waterfall, but it ³ _____ very far!
I ⁴ _____ in the lake. The water
was warm.
My sister ⁵ _____ a brown turtle.
She used her camera to take a photograph.
She ⁶ _____ a red crab, too. I don't like
crabs, so I'm glad I ⁷ _____ see the crab!
My mother ⁸ _____ a small fish in the lake.
But we ⁹ _____ eat it for lunch.
We ¹⁰ _____ sandwiches. We ¹¹ _____ water with
our lunch. It was a wonderful day.

3 **Read and complete the chart.**

My new school, by Jane

I went to my new school last month. It's a special school for dance. I live at school now. I visit my parents on weekends. At my new school, I have to be hardworking. I have to dance every morning and afternoon! I have to study at night. I'm very busy, but I love dancing. In school, I don't have to wash my clothes or clean the kitchen, but I have to make my bed. I never have to wash the dishes or take the trash out. It's great!

have to	don't have to
be hardworking	

4 **Look at activity 3. Write things that Jane *has to* / *doesn't have to* do.**

1 Jane has to be hardworking.

2

3

4

5 **(My World) Answer the questions about you.**

1 Where did you go on vacation last year?
We went to

2 What did you see and do?

3 Did you visit a museum?

4 What do you have to do on vacation?

5 What don't you have to do on vacation?

Feelings

1 **Read and complete the sentences. Use the words in the box.**

> roedb   yrang   rsspedriu   derasc   rrdieow   sythtri
> diter   ctixeed   ~~ngruhy~~   detresetni

1 I didn't eat breakfast this morning. I'm _____ *hungry* _____ .

2 He didn't drink any juice after the soccer game. He's _____ .

3 I watched this movie last year. I'm _____ .

4 She ran in the race. Now she's _____ .

5 I like my math class. I'm _____ in math.

6 My brother ate my ice cream! I'm _____ .

7 He didn't know about his birthday party. He was _____ .

8 She saw a snake in the cave. She was _____ .

9 Ben didn't study for the test. Now he's _____ .

10 We go on vacation tomorrow! I'm _____ .

2 **Look at activity 1. Complete the chart about you.**

What feelings do you have when you … ?

1 cry: *worried* _____

2 laugh: _____

3 skip: _____

4 shout: _____

5 do homework: _____

My picture dictionary ➔ **Go to page 91: Write the new words.**

3 Write sentences with *because*.

1 She's tired. She's cleaning the house.

She's tired because she's cleaning the house.

2 They're laughing. The book is funny.

_____

3 Ben's scared. He saw a shark.

_____

4 Liam's is shouting. He's angry.

_____

5 We're interested. The story is exciting.

_____

6 We're excited. We're going on vacation.

_____

4 Look and write sentences with *because*.

1 (girl / crying / dropped her ice cream)
The girl's crying because she dropped
her ice cream.

2 (dog / happy / it's eating the ice cream)

_____

_____

3 (Peter / hungry / breakfast time)

_____

4 (Tom / not hungry / tired)

_____

_____

5 (Karen / surprised / kayaking is easy)

_____

6 (Jane / worried / kayaking is difficult)

_____

5 Read and circle the correct words.

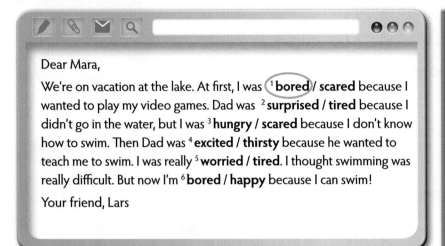

Dear Mara,

We're on vacation at the lake. At first, I was ¹**bored** / **scared** because I wanted to play my video games. Dad was ²**surprised** / **tired** because I didn't go in the water, but I was ³**hungry** / **scared** because I don't know how to swim. Then Dad was ⁴**excited** / **thirsty** because he wanted to teach me to swim. I was really ⁵**worried** / **tired**. I thought swimming was really difficult. But now I'm ⁶**bored** / **happy** because I can swim!

Your friend, Lars

Dear Lars,

That's wonderful. You learned to do something new!
Do you like the water now?
Do you want to go kayaking with me next weekend? Are you
⁷**interested** / **sad**?

Your friend, Mara

6 Put the words in order. Then complete the questions.

1 ___Why___ is Alex laughing? is / he's / Alex / because / watching / laughing / movie. / funny / a

Alex is laughing because he's watching a funny movie.

2 _____ is Katy hungry? she / hungry / lunch. / eat / She's / because / didn't

_____

3 _____ is Helen _____ ? because / she / tired / She's / played / volleyball.

_____

4 _____ is he _____ ? the / he's / excited / to / He's / movies. / because / going

_____

5 _____ she _____ ? can / ride / because / a / She's / bike. / happy / she

_____

6 _____ he _____ ? doesn't / He's / scared / he / because / like / bats.

_____

7 My World Ask and answer with a friend. Use the words in the box and your own ideas.

> happy   ~~tired~~   excited   interested   scared

> Why are you tired?   I'm tired because I played soccer.

8 **Read the story again and complete the sentences with the words in the box. Then number.**

[ ] **a** Jack needs help because of the _____ .

[ ] **b** Capu wants to _____ Jack and finds the annatto plant.

[1] **c** Capu's excited because he's in _South America_ .

[ ] **d** The children say _____ to Capu.

[ ] **e** The woman and girl use the plant to make a _____ .

goodbye
medicine
snake
~~South America~~
help

9 **Read and circle the correct words.**

1 Capuchin monkeys live in the … .
   a (rain forest)   **b** home   **c** medicine

2 The children are worried and scared because of the … .
   a rain forest   **b** snake   **c** annatto plant

3 What does Capu find on the tablet?
   a his family   **b** the annatto plant   **c** snakes

4 The rain forest people make medicine with … .
   a hospitals   **b** snakes   **c** plants

5 Why is Capu happy at the end?
   a because he likes medicine   **b** because he's hungry   **c** because he's home

10 **Read and circle the words that show the value: Respect nature.**

1 (Don't throw) / **Throw** bottles in the ocean.

2 **Don't take** / **Take** birds' nests.

3 **Don't put** / **Put** food in trash cans at the beach.

4 **Don't make** / **Make** fires in the forest.

5 **Litter** / **Don't litter** in the forest.

Story   Value

Skills: *Reading*

11 Read Milt's diary. Then use the underlined words to write sentences with *because*.

JUNE 6th

Today was a long day. We flew to Africa.
I was bored. The plane ride was ten hours!
I'm excited now. We're staying close to a national park!

JUNE 7th

Today we went to the national park. Lions climbed on our car, but we were safe in the car.
We also saw hippos in the river. They are so big! I'm surprised. Hippos are the most dangerous animals. It's not the lion! I'm hungry now. I didn't eat dinner. I was too excited.
I want to be a park guide. I am very interested in animals now.

1 _I was bored because the plane ride was ten hours._

2 _____

3 _____

4 _____

5 _____

12 Look at activity 11. Answer the questions.

1 What did Milt do on June 6th? _He flew to Africa._

2 Did Milt see lions on June 7th? _____

3 Why do you think Milt was safe on June 7th? _____

_____

4 Are hippos safe animals? _____

_____

5 Why was Milt too excited to eat dinner? _____

_____

13 **(TIP)** **How to talk about yesterday.**

When we write about yesterday, last week, and last year, we sometimes use *was* and *were*: *I was excited.   We were hungry.*

When we write about today, we sometimes use *am*, *is*, and *are* with the word *now*: *I'm excited now.   We're hungry now.*

Read Milt's diary again and:

1 circle the sentences with the word *now*.

2 draw boxes around the sentences with *was* and *were*.

Skills: *Writing*

14 **Think about your weekend or a vacation. Make notes about two things you did and your feelings.**

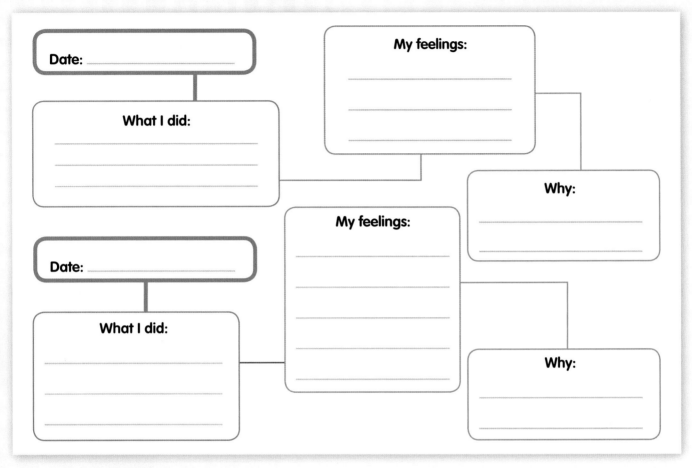

Date: _____

What I did:
_____
_____
_____

My feelings:
_____
_____

Why:
_____
_____

Date: _____

What I did:
_____
_____
_____

My feelings:
_____
_____
_____
_____
_____

Why:
_____
_____
_____

15 **Write two diary pages about your weekend or vacation.**

Date: _____

Date: _____

How do **animals communicate?**

1 **Think** Match the animals to how they communicate and their feelings.

1	bears	**a**	hiss		excited
2	wild cats	**b**	growl		happy
3	elephants	**c**	flap ears		angry
4	snakes	**d**	move heads		angry
5	polar bears	**e**	purr		happy

2 **Look at activity 1. Write sentences about how animals communicate their feelings.**

1 *Bears growl because they're angry.*

2 _____

_____

3 _____

_____

4 _____

_____

5 _____

_____

3 **Complete the chart with the words in the box.**

change color   flap ears   growl   hiss   purr
move fast   move head   touch hands

See	Hear
change color	*growl*

Evaluation

1 Complete the questions and put the words in order. Then match.

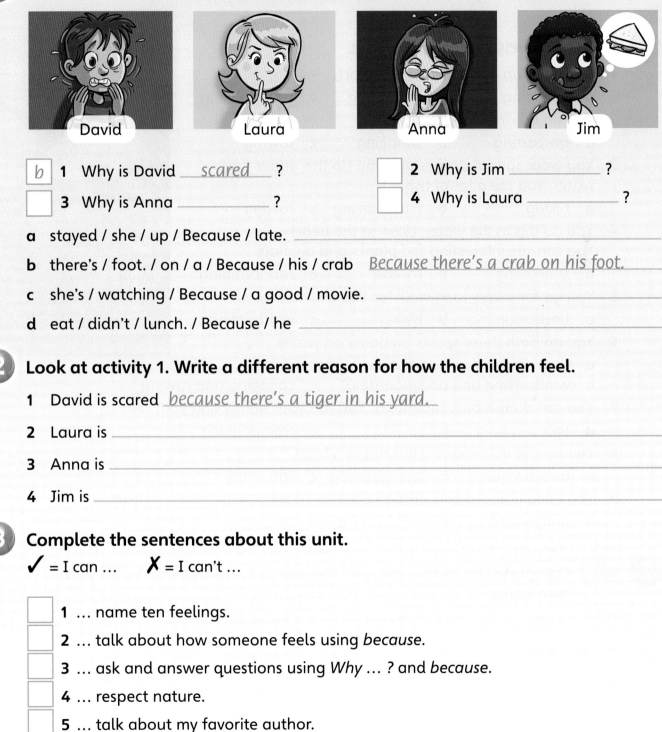

David   Laura   Anna   Jim

| b | **1** Why is David _____scared_____ ? | | | **2** Why is Jim _____ ? |
| | **3** Why is Anna _____ ? | | | **4** Why is Laura _____ ? |

a stayed / she / up / Because / late. _____

b there's / foot. / on / a / Because / his / crab   _Because there's a crab on his foot._

c she's / watching / Because / a good / movie. _____

d eat / didn't / lunch. / Because / he _____

2 Look at activity 1. Write a different reason for how the children feel.

1 David is scared _because there's a tiger in his yard._

2 Laura is _____

3 Anna is _____

4 Jim is _____

3 Complete the sentences about this unit.

✓ = I can …   ✗ = I can't …

☐ **1** … name ten feelings.

☐ **2** … talk about how someone feels using *because*.

☐ **3** … ask and answer questions using *Why … ?* and *because*.

☐ **4** … respect nature.

☐ **5** … talk about my favorite author.

6 The part of this unit I found the most interesting is _____ .

8 Outdoor sports

1 **Read and circle the correct words.**

1 You jump up and down in this sport.
  a canoeing **b** snorkeling **c** (trampolining)

2 You do this in a very small car.
  a go-carting **b** canoeing **c** rowing

3 You wear special clothes and you do this under the water. You see a lot of fish.
  a hiking **b** scuba diving **c** rowing

4 You do this in the water, close to the beach. You can see interesting sea plants and animals.
  a snorkeling **b** rowing **c** rock climbing

5 You go for a very long walk for this activity.
  a bodyboarding **b** hiking **c** windsurfing

6 You do both these sports on boats on water.
  a rock climbing and go-carting
  b windsurfing and bodyboarding **c** canoeing and rowing

7 You can do this on a mountain. You use your hands and your feet.
  a rock climbing **b** rowing **c** trampolining

8 You do this in the water, but not in a boat.
  a bodyboarding **b** trampolining **c** canoeing

9 You need a board and wind to do this.
  a bodyboarding **b** windsurfing **c** canoeing

2 **My World** **Complete the sentences. Use the words from activity 1 and your own ideas.**

1 I'd like to _____go canoeing_____ because _____.

2 I'd like to _____ because _____.

3 I'd like to _____ because _____.

4 I'd like to _____ because _____.

5 I'd like to _____ because _____.

My picture dictionary ➔ Go to page 92: Write the new words.

3 Look and write the sentences.

1	(Haley / rowing)	<u>Haley went rowing on Saturday.</u>
2	(she / windsurfing)	
3	(she / bodyboarding)	
4	(Fred / trampolining)	
5	(he / go-carting)	
6	(they / hiking)	

4 Look at activity 3. Complete the questions and write the answers.

1 _____Did_____ Haley _____go_____ scuba diving?   <u>No, she didn't.</u>

2 _____ Fred _____ rock climbing?

3 _____ they _____ bodyboarding?

4 _____ Fred _____ windsurfing?

5 _____ Haley _____ canoeing?

5 (My World) Answer the questions about you.

1 What did you do last Saturday?

<u>Last Saturday, I</u>

2 What did your friend do last weekend?

3 Did you go hiking last month?

4 Did you go to school last week?

6 Read and write the questions and answers.

	January	February	March	April	May
Jen	snowboarding	trampolining	windsurfing	rowing	go-carting

1 Paul: <u>When did you go windsurfing</u>   ?

Jen: <u>I went windsurfing in</u>   March.

2 Paul: _____ ?

Jen: _____ May.

3 Paul: _____ snowboarding?

Jen: _____ .

4 Paul: _____ rowing?

Jen: _____ .

5 Paul: _____ ?

Jen: _____ February.

	January	February	March	April	May
Eddie	hiking	rock climbing	windsurfing	canoeing	trampolining

	January	February	March	April	May
Kate	ice-skating	trampolining	rock climbing	windsurfing	canoeing

7 Read and complete the questions and answers.

Kate: ____<u>Did</u>____ you go windsurfing last year?

Eddie: Yes, ____<u>I did</u>____ .

Kate: So ____<u>did I</u>____ . _____ you _____ windsurfing?

Eddie: In _____ .

Kate: Oh, I _____ windsurfing in _____ .

Eddie: _____ you go canoeing?

Kate: Yes, _____ .

Eddie: So _____ . _____ you go _____ ?

Kate: I _____ in May.

Eddie: I see. I _____ canoeing in _____ .

8 (Think) **Read the story again. Match and then number.**

 1 The children are looking for __e__

   It's time for _____

   They fly back _____

   To get to the helicopter, they should _____

   They put on helmets _____

a to be safe.

b go rock climbing.

c Sofia to go home.

d to the library.

e something to fly.

9 **Use the words in the box to write answers.**

helicopter   goodbye   rock climbing   Colombia   the quiz

1 You can fly in this.   _____helicopter_____

2 You should use ropes and helmets to do this.   _____

3 Sofia comes from this place.   _____

4 The children got all the answers to win this.   _____

5 Sofia, Ruby, and Jack say this to each other.   _____

10 (My World) **Find and write sentences that show the value: Be safe.**

1 stop / Always / red / the / at / light.
    Always stop at the red light.

2 to / Learn / swim.
    _____

3 bike / Ride / your / slowly.
    _____

4 Don't / your / very / quickly. / food / eat
    _____

Story   Value   **77**

Skills: *Reading*

 11 **Look, read, and complete Tony's story. Use the words in the box.**

> bodyboarding   book   ~~swimming~~
> whale watching   swimming   windsurfing

My favorite day,

by Tony

My favorite day happened last July. My family and I went to the beach. They're all

sportier than me. My dad likes [1] __swimming__ . My sister likes [2] _____ .

My mom always goes [3] _____ . So they played sports, and I just read my

[4] _____ . I was so bored! The beach is not my favorite place.

Then I saw a man. He was really excited, and he pointed at the ocean. I looked at the ocean, and I

saw a tail! Then two tails! Then I used the man's special glasses called binoculars.

I saw whales [5] _____ in the ocean! I was really excited, too. Whales are very

big and very beautiful. They're so cool! Now I'm not bored at the beach because I love

[6] _____ !

12 **Look at activity 11. Answer the questions.**

1 When did Tony's favorite day happen?

   His favorite day happened last July.

2 What is Tony's family like?

   _____

3 Why was Tony bored?

   _____

4 Why was Tony excited?

   _____

5 Why do you think this was Tony's favorite day?

   _____

13 **(TIP)** **How to use *so*, *very*, and *really*.**

Use *so*, *very*, and *really* before words to make things bigger and stronger.
Add exclamation points if you want to:
This cake is really good!   *Tony is so nice!*   *That whale is really big!*

Read Tony's story again and circle the words that make things stronger.

Skills: *Writing*

14 **Think of a time you were *excited* or *interested*. Make notes about it.**

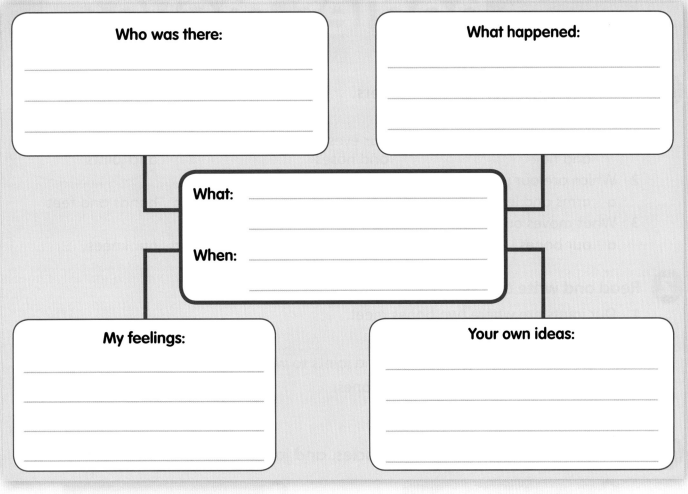

Who was there:

_____
_____
_____

What happened:

_____
_____
_____

What: _____
_____

When: _____
_____

My feelings:

_____
_____
_____
_____

Your own ideas:

_____
_____
_____
_____

15 **Write a story about the time you were *excited* or *interested*.**

Title: _____

_____
_____
_____
_____
_____
_____
_____
_____
_____

What makes our bodies move?

1 **Read and circle the correct answers.**

1 What makes our bodies move?
   - **a** our heads, faces, and hair
   - **b** our eyes, ears, and noses
   - **c** our bones, muscles, and joints
2 Which are our joints?
   - **a** arms and legs
   - **b** knees and elbows
   - **c** hands and feet
3 What moves our joints?
   - **a** our bones
   - **b** our muscles
   - **c** our knees

2 **Read and write _true_ or _false_.**

1 Our joints are where two bones meet.   _true_
2 There are no muscles in our legs.   _____
3 We need strong bones, muscles, and joints to watch TV.   _____
4 Our knees are between two arm bones.   _____
5 There are muscles in our faces.   _____

3 **Look and think. Which bones, muscles, and joints should be strong?**

Arm bones, muscles, and elbow joints.

Evaluation

1 Read and complete. Use the words in the box.

> didn't   February   hiking
> ~~went~~   windsurfing   When

Tina: Hi, Mike. Guess what! I ¹____went____ to Hawaii.

Mike: So did I. ²_____ did you go to Hawaii?

Tina: I went in ³_____ . It was hot.

Mike: I went in March. It was hotter. Did you go scuba diving?

Tina: No, I ⁴_____ . I went ⁵_____ .

Mike: Oh, I didn't go windsurfing. Did you go ⁶_____ ?

Tina: Yes, I did. I went hiking on a volcano!

2 Look at activity 1. Put the words in order. Then match to the answers.

1   Tina / When / go / Hawaii? / did / to
    When did Tina go to Hawaii? ⟨b⟩

2   Mike / to / in / Did / go / March? / Hawaii
    _____

3   the ocean? / What / Tina / did / do / in
    _____

4   go / Tina / Hawaii? / scuba diving / Did / in
    _____

5   do / What / volcano? / Tina / on / did / the
    _____

a   Yes, he did.

b   She went in February.

c   She went hiking.

d   No, she didn't.

e   She went windsurfing.

3 Complete the sentences about this unit.

✔ = I can …   ✗ = I can't …

☐ 1 … name ten outdoor sports.

☐ 2 … talk about activities people did last year or last month using *did* and *went*.

☐ 3 … ask and answer questions using *Did … ?* and *When did … ?*

☐ 4 … be safe.

☐ 5 … think and write about an unusual sport and how to play it.

6   My favorite part of this unit was _____ .

Review Units 7 and 8

1 **Find and circle the words in the box. Then complete the sentences.**

~~rowing~~   go-carting   interested   happy   ~~surprised~~
tired   hiking   sad   snorkeling   windsurfing

1 I'm _surprised_ that I liked _rowing_ .
   Usually I don't like boats. And I didn't like
   canoeing.

2 Iris was _____ last Friday because she
   didn't go _____ . She likes driving the
   little cars.

3 Mark wants to go _____ . He's
   _____ because he likes fish. He liked
   scuba diving, but he wants to try a new
   sport.

4 I'm _____ because I went
   _____ . I think it's more difficult than
   surfing or bodyboarding! I was excited
   because of the wind.

5 Jill is _____ because she went
   _____ on a mountain. She wants to
   go to bed.

S	N	O	R	K	E	L	I	N	G	K
G	O	C	A	R	T	I	N	G	F	X
B	H	A	P	P	Y	A	H	J	Q	T
W	I	Z	R	Y	F	N	N	K	M	Y
N	A	N	J	G	R	O	W	I	N	G
Z	S	U	R	P	R	I	S	E	D	D
T	I	N	T	E	R	E	S	T	E	D
X	T	I	R	E	D	Y	F	G	E	V
W	I	N	D	S	U	R	F	I	N	G
K	C	G	T	T	Z	S	A	D	N	W
C	D	E	E	H	I	K	I	N	G	G

2 **Read and match.**

1 They're laughing … | g | a Because he didn't study.

2 Nina is surprised … | | b She went trampolining.

3 Why is Leon worried? | | c They went last spring.

4 Why is Mary excited? | | d because there's a rabbit in the hat.

5 We didn't go … | | e Because it's her birthday.

6 What did Kyla do last Friday? | | f go-carting last Sunday.

7 When did they go swimming? | | g because the story is funny.

82

3 (Think) **Read and answer the questions.**

Four friends did four different activities last July:
Henry didn't go hiking, rock climbing, or bodyboarding.
Nancy didn't go rock climbing, canoeing, or hiking.
Mick didn't go canoeing, rock climbing, or bodyboarding.
Ellen didn't go bodyboarding, canoeing, or hiking.
The person who went canoeing was scared.
The person who went bodyboarding was excited.
The person who went rock climbing was interested.
The person who went hiking was happy.

1 Did Henry go rock climbing last July?

No, he didn't. He went canoeing.

2 Did Nancy go bodyboarding last July?

_____

3 What did Mick do last July?

_____

4 What did Ellen do last July?

_____

5 Who was scared last July? Why?

_____

6 Who was excited last July? Why?

_____

4 (My World) **Answer the questions about you.**

1 What are you feeling now and why?
I'm feeling _____

2 Is your friend happy? Why or why not?

_____

3 What did you do last December?

_____

4 Do you like swimming in the ocean?

_____

5 What activities would you like to do?

_____

Around the world

_____

_____

_____

_____

_____

_____

_____

_____

_____

_____

1 Family and pets

2 On the playground

4 Gadgets

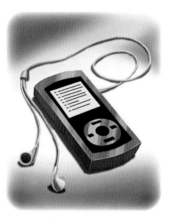

6 Helping at home

8 Outdoor sports

Story fun

1 Who said it? Read and write the names.

Jack   Ruby   Sofia

1 _____*Sofia*_____   Oh, no! I don't like bats!

2 _____   It's 1950. Look at this diary.

3 _____   And look at this! It's a message!

4 _____   It was the key.

5 _____   OK, but we should be safe. Put on your helmets and follow me.

6 _____   And look! It's the monkey!

7 _____   Quick! Help me find some shells.

8 _____   Yes! They made a medicine with the plant.

9 _____   My pen pal, Sofia, is from Colombia! We can email her.

2 Look at the pictures and write the values.

> Encourage your friends. Use technology wisely. Learn about other cultures.
>
> Be kind to animals. Help other people. ~~Be safe.~~

1

Come on, kids!

Hold on tight to the ropes.

Be safe.

2

What's wrong?

The King wants to visit today. We have to finish the palace!

We can help.

3

Oh, dear! I'm not good at acting.

You're a great actor, Jack!

Action!

4

The first question is about the flower festival.

Yes … ?

Where are we?

5

Look at this poor monkey. His name's Capu.

Let's give him some fruit.

6

Let's use these blankets.

I'll ask for help. I can use the tablet.

Look and complete the word puzzle.

Across

1 Do trees grow in Antarctica?

2 Which city in Colombia has a flower festival?

3 Where does the annatto plant grow?

Down

4 Where are capuchin monkeys from?

5 Which country is Hollywood in?

6 Which river flows through Egypt?

7 What is a dolphin family called?

Thanks and Acknowledgments

The authors and publishers would like to thank the following contributors:

Blooberry Design: concept design, book design, page make-up
Bridget Kelly: editing
Lisa Hutchins: freelance editing
John Marshall Media: audio recording and production
hyphen S.A.: publishing management, American English edition

The authors and publishers acknowledge the following sources of copyright material and are grateful for the permissions granted. Although every effort has been made, it has not always been possible to identify the sources of all the material used or to trace all copyright holders. If any omissions are brought to our notice, we will be happy to include the appropriate acknowledgments on reprinting.

The authors and publishers would like to thank the following illustrators:

Pablo Gallego (Beehive Illustration): pp. 3, 7, 15, 23, 33, 41, 51, 59, 69, 77, 93, 94, 95; Mark Duffin: pp. 4, 55, 75; Paul Williams (Syvie Poggio): pp. 19, 33; Timo Grubbing (Beehive): pp. 26, 67; Dusan Pavlic (Beehive): pp. 27, 31, 56, 73; Simon Walmesley: pp. 29, 63; Ilias Arahovitis (Beehive): pp. 30, 60; Humberto Blanco (Sylvie Poggio): pp. 64, 78; Brian Lee: pp. 36, 62, 70; Richard Jones (Beehive): p. 37; Niall Harding (Beehive): p. 54; Gustavo Berardo (Beehive): p. 58; Hardinge (Monkey Feet): pp. 84, 85, 86, 87, 88, 89, 90, 91, 92.

The authors and publishers would like to thank the following for permission to reproduce photographs:

p. 4 (opener): Tim Gainey/Alamy; p. 5 (1): Digital Media Pro/Shutterstock; p. 5 (2): Blend Images/Shutterstock; p. 5 (3): JGI/Tom Grill/Corbis; p. 5 (4): Kamira/Shutterstock; p. 6: Tony Garcia/Corbis; p. 7: imageBROKER/Alamy; p. 8 (T): Basque Country - Mark Baynes/Alamy; p. 8 (B): Geoffrey Robinson/Alamy; p. 10 (opener): John Dunne/Getty; p. 10 (a): BRUCE COLEMAN INC./Alamy; p. 10 (b): Sue Martin/Alamy; p. 10 (c): Dario Sabljak/Shutterstock; p. 11: Jaren Jai Wicklund/Shutterstock; p. 12 (opener): Wilfried Martin/Getty; p. 12 (TR): VP Photo Studio/Shutterstock; p. 12 (1): H. Mark Weidman Photography/Alamy; p. 12 (2): PathDoc/Shutterstock; p. 12 (3): oliveromg/Shutterstock; p. 12 (4): Wavebreak Media LTD/Corbis; p. 13 (TL): Donna Ellen Coleman/Shutterstock; p. 13 (TR): Brocreative/Shutterstock; p. 14: Muellek Josef/Shutterstock; p. 15: John Warburton-Lee Photography/Alamy; p. 16 (T): Volodymyr Burdiak/Shutterstock; p. 16 (B): Dorothy Alexander/Alamy; p. 18 (opener): TeguhSantosa/Getty; p. 18 (a): Nature Picture Library/Alamy; p. 18 (b): david tipling/Alamy; p. 18 (c): Christina Krutz/Corbis; p. 20 (opener): J. McPhail/Shutterstock; p. 20 (a): Grady Reese/Corbis; p.

20 (b): Alex Segre/Alamy; p. 20 (c): Paul Springett 02/Alamy; p. 20 (d): Bokhach/Shutterstock; p. 20 (e): Giulio_Fornasar/Shutterstock; p. 20 (f): SergiyN/Shutterstock; p. 21: Agencja Fotograficzna Caro/Alamy; p. 22 (T): Ronnie Kaufman/Larry Hirshowitz/Corbis; p. 22 (B): Hero Images Inc./Alamy; p. 23: Markus Mainka/Shutterstock; p. 24: luminaimages/Shutterstock; p. 28 (a): takayuki/Shutterstock; p. 28 (b): Susan Schmitz/Shutterstock; p. 28 (c): Cristian Zamfir/Shutterstock; p. 28 (d): S Curtis/Shutterstock; p. 30 (opener): Michael Moxter/Getty; p. 30 (1): Jason Edwards/Getty; p. 30 (2): David Osborn/Alamy; p. 30 (3): Bryce R. Bradford/Getty; p. 30 (4): Steve Hamblin/Alamy; p. 30 (5): James Azzurro/Alamy; p. 32 (a): Johan Swanepoel/Shutterstock; p. 32 (b): davemhuntphotography/Shutterstock; p. 32 (c): imageBROKER/Alamy; p. 32 (d): Maros Bauer/Shutterstock; p. 34: Egill Bjarnason/Alamy; p. 36 (opener): Zac Macaulay/Corbis; p. 38 (opener): Scott Stulberg/Corbis; p. 38 (T): Ralko/Shutterstock; p. 38 (B): Andersen Ross/Getty; p. 39 (1): wavebreakmedia/Shutterstock; p. 39 (2): Fotokostic/Shutterstock; p. 39 (3): Happy person/Shutterstock; p. 39 (4): Pauline St. Denis/Corbis; p. 39 (5): gorillaimages/Shutterstock; p. 39 (6): holbox/Shutterstock; p. 40 (T): Sergey Novikov/Shutterstock; p. 40 (B): www.saint-tropez-photo.com/Getty; p. 41: Andresr/Shutterstock; p. 42 (1): Science Museum/Science and Society Picture Library; p. 42 (2): Science & Society Picture Library/Getty; p. 44: All Canada Photos/Alamy; p. 45: Ruslan Guzov/Shutterstock; p. 46 (1): Isabelle Kuehn/Shutterstock; p. 46 (2): Steve Noakes/Shutterstock; p. 46 (3): igor.stevanovic/Shutterstock; p. 46 (4): Andaman/Shutterstock; p. 46 (4): Stefan Pircher/Shutterstock; p. 46 (5): Photoshot Holdings Ltd/Alamy; p. 46 (6): imageBROKER/Alamy; p. 48 (opener): George Steinmetz/Corbis; p. 48 (T): Calin Tatu/Shutterstock; p. 48 (B): VVO/Shutterstock; p. 49 (TL): bikeriderlondon/Shutterstock; p. 49 (TR): gorillaimages/Shutterstock; p. 50: KayaMe/Shutterstock; p. 51: MANDY GODBEHEAR/Shutterstock; p. 52 (T): Whit Richardson/Alamy; p. 52 (B): Holger Leue/Getty; p. 54: Corey Ford/Stocktrek Images/Getty; p. 56: Jupiterimages/Getty; p. 57 (T): Yarinca/Getty; p. 57 (B): Blend Images - KidStock/Getty; p. 59: Blend Images/Alamy; p. 62: Weyers, L./Corbis; p. 64 (1): VVO/Shutterstock; p. 64 (2): Janne Hamalainen/Shutterstock; p. 64 (3): Galyna Andrushko/Shutterstock; p. 64 (4): Marques/Shutterstock; p. 64 (5): Petr Kopka/Shutterstock; p. 64 (6): Catmando/Shutterstock; p. 64 (7): haraldmuc/Shutterstock; p. 64 (8): Kevin Eaves/Shutterstock; p. 64 (9): Jason Patrick Ross/Shutterstock; p. 66 (opener): Chad Slattery/Getty; p. 66 (B): Brand New Images/Getty; p. 67 (TR) Pete Pahham/Shutterstock; p. 69: Blend Images/Alamy; p. 72 (opener): Randy Wells/Corbis; p. 72 (BR): Roblan/Shutterstock; p. 74 (opener): mountainberryphoto/Getty; p. 74 (BR): Jeremy Pembrey/Alamy; p. 77: Beth Swanson/Shutterstock; p. 80 (opener): John P Kelly/Getty; p. 80 (1): BSIP SA/Alamy; p. 80 (2): CroMary/Shutterstock; p. 80 (3): Aurora Photos/Alamy; p. 80 (4): Arthur Tilley/Getty; p. 81: tomas del amo/Shutterstock; p. 82: Hero Images/Corbis; p. 83: Philip Quirk/Alamy.

Front Cover photo by aghezzi/Getty Images